B. Cole sculp.ᵗ

the famous Poet Shakespear was Born.

Linda —
    Shakespeare in
modern English or, what
his stories really mean
to you.
                    Arvida
                    ('73)

Nicolas
BENTLEY'S
tales from
SHAKESPEARE

Nicolas
BENTLEY'S
tales from
SHAKESPEARE

SIMON AND SCHUSTER NEW YORK

First U.S. printing
SBN 671-21500-0
Library of Congress Catalog Card Number: 72 93013
Printed and bound in Great Britain
by Cox and Wyman Ltd, Fakenham

To
Arabella

> 'Tis my familiar sin
> With maids to seem the lapwing and to jest.
>
> MEASURE FOR MEASURE

Contents

Illustrations

Colour plates

Preface

It has been my endeavour throughout this work to reflect the high moral tone of Charles and Mary Lamb's *Tales from Shakespeare*. It was their aim, so they said, to explain the plots of the plays to 'very young children', and in so far as they managed to do this with scarcely a hint of murder, incest, illegitimacy, blackmail, transvestism, hallucinatory drugs, grievous bodily harm and other features with which the plays abound, they may be said to have done pretty well.

The very young child in those days was obviously a different specimen from the very young child of today, and not merely because it never knew the delights of watching scenes of bloodshed, violence and cruelty on TV, or enjoyed the benefits of a third-rate state education, or the ceaseless love and care of a baby-sitter, but because its understanding seems to have been superior to that of the twentieth-century chickadee. Or was it wishful thinking on the Lambs' part that led them to suppose a five-year-old would take in its stride the meaning of thoughts ascribed to Ophelia in these words: 'She compared the faculties of his once noble mind and excellent understanding, impaired as they were with the deep melancholy that oppressed him, to sweet bells which in themselves are capable of most exquisite music'? So much for the proverbial innocence of the Lamb.

However, others besides very young children sometimes feel the need for an explanation of Shakespeare's stories. The element of coincidence is often so staggering, and so incomprehensible the blatant disregard of the obvious, that a certain amount of mystification is understandable. Nor are modern producers always helpful in clarifying the plot. I do not want to decry experimental productions, without which the theatre would be as dull as a Church of England service—or perhaps I go too far. Let us say not quite as dull. However, the purpose of experiment must surely be either proof or discovery, yet sometimes I find it hard to make out what an experimental producer has proved that was only suspected before or discovered that was hitherto unknown. The complexity of Hamlet's character is not easy to understand and is not made easier, for me, at any rate, if the play is performed on a stage devoid of all properties except a tea-chest wrapped in aluminium foil. Nor do the costumes of du Maurier's era help me to find a deeper significance or a greater beauty in *The Merchant of Venice*.

It is for those, like myself, who sometimes find it difficult to follow or to remember exactly what is supposed to be going on, that I have ventured upon these outlines of Shakespeare's plots.

In telling their *Tales* the Lambs cheated a bit, sometimes altering the time sequence in the interests of lucidity and even cutting out certain characters altogether. But *Twelfth Night* without Malvolio, as in the Lambs' version, seems to me as poor a thing as *Hamlet* without the Prince of Denmark, so here I have rectified several of the omissions the Lambs thought fit to make.

Some of the stories, divested of actions that may have immediate significance on the stage, do occasionally seem to need a little clarification, and in most of these cases I have stuck to the Lambs' sequence of events. And just as the Lambs' idiom was that of their own day, so I have tried to reinterpret the stories for modern readers in the idiom to which they are accustomed.

The plays are full of sub-plots, often more complicated than the plays themselves, but since some of these sub-plots tend to get confused with the main stories, I have with reluctance left out most of them.

Not all the plays are included here. I have omitted the historical dramas and also a few of the less well-known plays, as did the Lambs. The stories of the historical plays are more familiar than some of the others because they bear traces of events recorded at the time and of which we learn at school. Moreover, the historical plays seem on the whole less confusing than some, such as *Measure for Measure* or *All's Well that Ends Well*, where even before the first interval, the mind, unless conditioned to the intricacies of the Shakespearean plot, is inclined to boggle.

There are some admirers of Shakespeare who think it

idolatrous to treat his plays as anything but holy writ. I am not one of these. My deep and abiding love of Shakespeare does not blind me to what must seem in this day and age imperfections in some of his plots, with their labyrinthine construction and frequent improbabilities. In any case, it is not with the mechanics of the drama that Shakespeare was chiefly concerned, but with the mechanics of the human mind, and about that he knew as much as was ever discovered by Freud, over whom he had the inestimable advantage of having a sense of humour. If the stunted embryo of such a sense lurked somewhere in the recesses of Freud's mind, I doubt that it would have enabled him to see a joke against himself. Shakespeare, I am quite sure, knew no such inhibition, and it is in this belief and with apologies to his memory that I present these tales.

Nicolas BENTLEY'S tales from SHAKESPEARE

Macbeth

The perils of the social climber have never been more
faithfully delineated than in *Macbeth*. In the character of
Lady Macbeth, Shakespeare created a classic type of social
snob, though one which is happily less familiar nowadays
than in his own time.

At the opening of the play, three elderly women are trying
to decide when and where they shall next meet. Macbeth
and Banquo, returning from the wars, happen to pass the
spot where they are clacketting and Macbeth in his lordly
way gives them a civil greeting.

One of the women, somewhat to his surprise, as he is
miles away from the Balmoral estate where he lives, greets
him as Thane of Glamis, which is the quaint Scottish title
by which he is known. Another greets him as Thane of
Cawdor, which Macbeth puts down to the poor old thing
being a bit mixed up. The third woman hails him as 'King
that shall be hereafter', which is frankly ridiculous, or so he
thinks at the time.

Then the women turn to Banquo and in a rather round-
about way imply to his astonishment (the thought never
having entered his head) that although he himself will not
become king, his heirs will eventually do so. The three
women are then obliterated by the sudden clamping down
of a Scotch mist, which is probably just as well, because
Macbeth, having not the ghost of a sense of humour, is
always ready to suspect that people are trying to be funny
at his expense.

Well, you can imagine his absolute amazement when five
minutes later a King's Messenger comes rushing up with
the news that the King has been graciously pleased to confer
on him the Thaneship of Cawdor. Being, like his wife, a
snob, and a Scottish snob at that, which is the furthest
limit to which snobbery can go, Macbeth is absolutely
overjoyed. He tears home and tells all to Lady Macbeth,
who being exceedingly ambitious socially, says that they
must take immediate steps to see that Clause III of the
elderly women's prophecy is fulfilled. But Macbeth says,
no, they can't possibly do that as it would involve blood-

Thou sure and firm-set earth,
Hear not my steps . . .

shed, meaning the doing in of his beloved kinsman, King Duncan. His wife, however, a woman with nerves of steel and utterly unscrupulous, says that such talk makes her puke, and she begins to consider by what means she can attain her vile ends.

At this juncture providence plays straight into her hands, because King Duncan decides to embark on a royal progress through his domains and announces his imminent descent on the Macbeths with his two sons, Malcolm and Donalbain.

Lady Macbeth, all sweetness and light, receives the news with mixed though well-disguised feelings. She is in absolute ecstasies, of course, at having a reigning monarch as a house guest, but at the same time she can't wait to see him escorted off the premises, feet first.

The King, on his arrival, having had rather a hard day, decides to make an early night of it, and as soon as he is tucked in, two grooms are posted outside the bedroom door in case he wants a drink of water or to go to the john. (Not even the simplest bodily function could be performed by royalty in those days without some degree of ceremony.)

Lady Macbeth, having spent the afternoon perfecting her evil plan, has now got the whole thing taped. She is in such a state of impatience to place the royal diadem on her own lily-white brow that she decides to do the deed herself, knowing Macbeth for the cowardly poltroon that he is behind a façade of old-world politeness and ancestral pride.

Having seen to it that both the King's servants are well and truly plastered, she creeps into his chamber with a breadknife and is just about to dunk it into Duncan, when a totally out-of-character metamorphosis occurs. Looking at the King, flat on his back, mouth wide open and snoring so that the arras round the bed billows like a mainsail, she is reminded for some reason or other of Daddy, to whom, though he was only a small-time laird, she was always devoted. At this crucial moment her determination fails her and she goes back to Macbeth and tells him to get on with it.

After a bit of argument, he agrees. He takes the knife

17

and goes up to the King's bedroom, but by this time he is in such a state of nerves himself that the slightest thing makes him jump and he keeps imagining he is seeing things. He even makes a grab at an imaginary dagger in the air, but of course there is nothing there, so he goes on upstairs feeling rather a fool.

He marches into the King's bedroom, pins him to the pillow with a well-aimed thrust, and then walks straight out again, dripping with blood. By a strange coincidence, just as he is coming out of the room, one of the two drunks lying in the passage has a nightmare and shouts out 'Murder!', to which the other one, also more or less unconscious, answers, 'God bless us!' Macbeth would fain cap this with 'Amen', but feels that that would be a bit much.

He totters back to Lady Macbeth, who, being a woman of good sense in spite of her shortcomings, tells him to go and wash his hands. While he is in the bathroom, she goes upstairs again to the late King's chamber—by this time she has quite recovered herself—and, cool as a cucumber, she wipes the knife on the senseless visages of the two drunks lying outside the bedroom.

Well, of course, when the King's breakfast is taken up the next morning and the dirty deed discovered, all Hell is let loose. A hideous trumpet calls to parley the sleepers of the house, like a division bell ringing in the Commons, and everyone dashes madly about the place. Malcolm and Donalbain, having a pretty shrewd suspicion that they are probably the next in line for Lady Macbeth's attentions, clear out post haste, leaving Macbeth to claim their father's throne, which he does almost before they have shut the front door.

Theoretically everything should now be smooth running, but Lady Macbeth is bothered by the old women's allusion in Scene 1, Act 1 to Banquo's son inheriting the throne instead of her own offspring. She decides to take no chances, so poor old Banquo is chalked up as next on the list.

Dissimulation being, as you might say, Lady Macbeth's

middle name (which in reality was probably Fiona, Charlotte, Lavinia, or some such upper-class moniker) she gets up a dinner party, ostensibly in honour of Banquo and his son Fleance (known in the family circle as the Flea). On their way to the party, on secret instructions from Macbeth, Banquo and the Flea are set upon by some Gaelic thugs and Banquo is slaughtered, but the Flea does a flit. Macbeth then has the effrontery to say to the assembled guests that he can't think what's keeping the other two. But soon his conscience, such as it is, raises its ugly little head and suddenly he sees Banquo's ghost, an apparition invisible to the rest of the company. He staggers back, like one to whom Paul Getty's income tax demand has been sent by mistake, and reels round the table mouthing and gesticulating. Lady Macbeth, fearful lest some indiscretion might feature in Macbeth's maunderings, explains that he goes off like this from time to time and begs them all to excuse him. And so the party breaks up.

The Macbeths now begin to exhibit neurotic symptoms of guilt. Macbeth himself gets into such a state that he decides there's nothing for it but to go in search of the old women he met in Act 1 and ask them precisely what they were driving at in uttering their mysterious prophecies. So he makes for a blasted heath somewhere in the country where he knows the women sometimes go for a picnic and finds them preparing a *ragout*, the ingredients of which, as described by the old ladies, sound perfectly disgusting. Macbeth asks to be put in direct touch with the trio's spirit controls, and this is instantly arranged. It is then seen that the first woman's control suffers from a pensionable disability; it has only a head. This warns Macbeth against Macduff, the Thane of Fife. Macbeth says thanks very much, then he accosts the second woman's control, a small child covered in blood. This little kiddy tells Macbeth not to give a damn for anyone. 'Be bloody, bold and resolute.' 'Right, I will,' says Macbeth, and he resolves then and there to do Macduff in at the first opportunity.

The third control is another little kiddy, this time

wearing a crown and humping a tree about, as if in practice for tossing the caber. He tells Macbeth not to worry. Only if he should ever hear that Birnam Wood has come to Dunsinane will he know that his number is up. Well, the idea of a complete forest going for a cross-country ramble is so ludicrous that Macbeth laughs the idea to scorn, even exclaiming in the extremity of his mirth, 'Sweet bodements!', which has them all doubled up.

Then eight phantom kings come marching along in Indian file, followed by Banquo's ghost, who grins at Macbeth, pointing at this ghostly octet to indicate that they will be the ones to inherit Macbeth's throne.

Macbeth is furious, but worse is to follow. As soon as he gets home, he hears that Macduff has got together an army of freedom fighters and is on the march. So he gives orders that all Macduff's relatives, nearest and dearest, uncles, aunts, in-laws, the lot, shall be put to the sword, and he indeed must be a villain without scruple who would put his friend's aunt to the sword.

Meanwhile Lady Macbeth has her big scene. Under the compulsion of her guilt complex she has taken to sleep-walking, and now, watched by her doctor and her maid, she drifts round the house talking to herself; but unlike your ordinary somnambulist she talks in blank verse. The gist of her remarks is that somehow she has got some blood on her hands and although she has tried every known form of detergent she can't get the stuff off. But as neither the doctor nor the maid have the slightest suspicion of what's been happening, they can't make head or tail of what she is talking about and just stand there whispering and shaking their heads like a couple of old grannies. Well, eventually Lady Macbeth dies in circumstances that indicate the possibility of suicide, and a good thing too.

While all this has been going on, Macduff, with Malcolm as his second-in-command, has been marching hot-foot towards Dunsinane. Macduff, an ex-camouflage officer in a previous border skirmish, orders his men to hew down the branches of some trees and use these for their concealment,

She has spoke what she should not, I am sure of that

with the result that when one of Macbeth's look-outs sees them advancing, the poor fish thinks Birnam Wood is on the move and rushes screaming this dread news to Macbeth.

Macbeth now realises that he has had it, but he decides to put up a fight all the same and in due course fetches up face to face with his accursed enemy. 'Lay on, Macduff!' he cries, to which Macduff responds by giving him a series of tremendous thwacks, so that ere long Macbeth changes his tune and starts yelling 'Lay off, Macduff!' But not a bit of it. Macduff, absolutely berserk by this time, swipes Macbeth's head clean off his shoulders—unfortunately this almost always occurs off-stage—and then with a rather bizarre sense of generosity, picks up the severed pate and presents it to Malcolm, who after a short speech of thanks, ascends the throne amid the plaudits of the few remaining clansmen who have enough strength left to clap.

The Tempest

The situation in *The Tempest* is one that is not unfamiliar in our own day. It concerns the betrayal of a simple and retiring character by a ruthless combine bent on achieving its own ends.

One of the things that is difficult to understand about the play is why Prospero, who is a magician and therefore should be able to command a fairly decent standard of living, deliberately chooses to go and live in a cave. This he has done after being shipwrecked on a lonely island with his daughter Miranda, who when the play opens is fifteen, though prematurely advanced for her age.

It is necessary to understand at the outset that Prospero, as well as having magical powers, is also the rightful Duke of Milan. Not long before his arrival on the island, its only inhabitants had been a woman called Sycorax (now dead) and her mentally-handicapped son Caliban, whose survival presents a striking argument in favour of controlled euthanasia. By one of those coincidences so invaluable to the development of Shakespeare's plots, Sycorax had also possessed magical powers, which she had used to imprison various sprites in the trunks of some trees, on the dubious pretext that the little creatures had disregarded her whims. Prospero immediately counteracts this move by releasing these unfortunate juveniles from their arboreal confinement. The leading sprite, known as Ariel, is, as a matter of fact, a rather tiresome and inquisitive little urchin, who spends much of his time tormenting the unfortunate Caliban, whose defects render him useless for all but performance of the simplest menial tasks.

One day, for the entertainment of Miranda, who is absolutely bored stiff with hanging about in the cave, Prospero decides to cause a tremendous hurricane, during which a ship is driven onto the shores of the island. Now Prospero, the crafty old conjuror, has discovered by some occult means that the passenger list includes the names of a number of people he knows, among them his brother Antonio, who has usurped his dukedom, the King of Naples, and the King's son, Ferdinand. This tempest business is really tit for tat, because the reason Prospero came to be on the island in the first place was that twelve years earlier Antonio, sick of Prospero's studious mien and introspective character, had set him and the puling Miranda adrift in an open boat.

All this Prospero now tells Miranda, and then he gives her a poke with his wand and sends her off into a trance so that she shan't overhear him talking to Ariel, because Ariel being invisible to everyone except Prospero, the old boy feels understandably embarrassed about being seen talking as if to the empty air.

He has sent Ariel off to see how things have been going on, and now the lad comes haring back to say that the shipwreck has been a huge success. Antonio and the King were at first petrified out of their wits and Ferdinand was so scared that he jumped overboard. None of them ever expected to see each other again (this, of course, was part of Prospero's cunning scheme) and now Ariel sets off to bring Ferdinand along.

Well, when Miranda catches sight of him—don't forget that Prospero is the only thing in trousers she has ever seen, not counting Caliban, who is neither one thing nor the other—she goes out of her mind. Ferdinand is no less pleased with the sight of Miranda, so Prospero, observing this, devises an ingenious test with a view to deciding his eligibility as a son-in-law. He proposes that Ferdinand shall have his hands and neck tied together and in this unconventional posture shall subsist for an unspecified time on a diet of withered roots, husks, acorns and shell-fish, washed down with a little salt water. If he survives this Prospero reckons he will be able to survive pretty well anything.

Ferdinand's answer to this proposal may well be imagined, and upon hearing it Prospero waves his wand over him, with the result that Ferdinand becomes powerless to move except when Prospero gives him orders. He is instructed to start stacking some timber, and in a frenzied outburst of energy he builds up an enormous pile, at the same time carrying on an animated conversation with

I'll swear upon that bottle to be thy true subject

Miranda about sex. Prospero, overhearing them, decides they must be in love, which was exactly what he had intendéd. In spite of his professed fondness for the simple life, he has a keen eye for the main chance, and not every old person who lives in a cave sees an opportunity for his only daughter to marry into a royal house. True, it was only the royal house of Naples in this case, but Prospero has rather exalted visions of claiming, however indirectly, some tincture of the blood royal.

Meanwhile the rest of the party, have been wandering about in a vacant sort of way, looking for somewhere to have a meal. Antonio's butler, Stephano, who made sure of his liquor before abandoning ship, is as tight as a tick, when he comes across Caliban collecting firewood in the forest. Caliban, whose experience of the human race is somewhat limited, is entranced by this besotted manservant, whom he conducts to Prospero's cave.

By this time the others, fagged to death and half starved, suddenly find themselves confronted through Prospero's magic with an enormous banquet and are just about to launch into the *saumon fumé* when a maddening thing occurs. A pterodactyl suddenly appears and wolfs the lot. The creature then gives Antonio and the King a dressing down for the way they have treated Prospero and Miranda, and both of them apologise.

Ariel, who as usual has been hanging about listening to what was being said, hurries back and tells Prospero, who bids him fetch the party to his humble abode. As soon as they turn up, Prospero says to them, 'Look—' and he opens a door in the cave and there are Ferdinand and Miranda. And can you guess what they're up to? Well, you're wrong. They're playing chess, believe it or not.

Prospero now invites the whole assembly to stay to dinner (little do they know that Caliban is doing the cooking). 'And for your evening's entertainment,' he says 'I will relate the story of my life'. Of course it's too late now for them to say they can't stay, but seeing what Antonio did to Prospero in the first place, it serves them right.

I have no ambition
To see a goodlier man

After dinner, Prospero takes leave of Ariel, who wants to try his luck as a free-lance sprite, and then he buries his wand, having decided to give up magic. And so they all depart for Naples, sailing into the sunset to the strains of *Funiculi funicula*.

Twelfth Night

If you can believe in the possibility of identical twins, male and female, being so alike as to be literally indistinguishable, you will believe anything—even the plot of *Twelfth Night*.

The twins in this case, Sebastian and Viola, are voyaging in the Adriatic when their ship sinks. Viola is rescued by an old sea dog, but Sebastian's fate is not disclosed. It so happens that Viola lands on a part of the Dalmatian coast which the old sea dog knows well. He also knows the local big shot, Orsino, who has got a tremendous crush on a girl called Olivia, but she won't look at him.

Olivia, unhinged by the recent death of her brother, has adopted this as a pretext for withdrawing from the world and abjuring male society for seven years—the reverse of the seven-year-itch.

Viola, who believes her own brother to be dead, has also become a bit eccentric, though in a different way. Nothing will satisfy her but to serve Orsino as a page—not that she has ever clapped eyes on him—and with the old sea dog's help she lands the job. The old man also humours her to the extent of providing her, on her insistence, with an outfit exactly like Sebastian's. Eccentricity could hardly be carried further, but then without this device nor could the plot.

Orsino takes quite a fancy to his new page, who goes by the name of Cesario. With a remarkable lack of discretion, as between master and servant, Orsino tells Cesario every detail of his wooing of Olivia, moaning and groaning about it for hours on end. Cesario, flattered at being taken into Orsino's confidence in this way, falls passionately in love with him, but of course daren't say anything because of the idiotic masquerade she has embarked on. To make matters worse, Orsino presently decides to have another go at Olivia and sends Cesario round to her as a sort of envoy.

Well, you can imagine Cesario's feelings, so the more credit to her that she persists in hanging about until Olivia consents to see her. And when eventually she does consent —bingo! Olivia falls in love with *her*. In fact, so besotted is

Not black in my mind, though yellow in my legs

she that as soon as Cesario has left her, she sends her steward, Malvolio, scuttling after her with a ring, making out that it was one that Cesario had brought her as a gift from Orsino. The transparent imbecility of this move makes it clear to Cesario that Olivia must be in love with her.

Meanwhile, Olivia's servants, who can't stand Malvolio,, decide to improve on nature by making him an even bigger fool than he appears to be. While he is stalking about in the shrubbery, he picks up a letter, unsigned but apparently from Olivia, making it plain that she loves him and urging him to give her some reciprocal signs when they next meet, *ie*, by sporting yellow stockings (which no man of fashion would disgrace his calves by wearing) and letting it show in his visage that he understands what she is after.

Now, when Cesario tells Orsino about the meeting with Olivia, he still refuses to take no for an answer and sends Cesario back again, and this time, instead of her having to hang about outside the house, the doors are thrown open and Olivia makes her as welcome as the sun in mid-winter.

But again Olivia sends Orsino a dusty answer. On the way to deliver it, Cesario is challenged by an extraordinary individual called Aguecheek, a pathetic specimen who, like Orsino, is in love with Olivia and imagines Cesario to be a rival, having seen the two of them chasing each other round Olivia's orchard.

At the moment, another sea dog called Antonio (no relation to Prospero in *The Tempest*) intervenes on Cesario's behalf. Cesario is naturally rather surprised, not having the faintest idea who he is. As a matter of fact, he is a friend and benefactor of young Sebastian, whom he fished out of the Adriatic when their ship went down and to whom he has just lent his purse. Mistaking Cesario for Sebastian, Antonio asks her to let him have it back again. Cesario, of course, denies ever having seen his wretched purse and on this rather uncomfortable note the scene is brought to a close by Antonio suddenly being pounced upon by several of Orsino's aides, who arrest him on a cock-and-bull charge of having wounded some relation of Orsino's years earlier.

Getting back to Olivia, she at this time is doing a bit of gardening when suddenly Malvolio appears, dressed in hideous yellow stockings and leering and grimacing like a maniac. Assuming this to be not far from the truth, Olivia backs hurriedly indoors, telling the servants to deal with him, but to treat him gently.

Meanwhile, Sebastian, mooching round the town, is challenged by the half-witted Aguecheek, who thinks he is Cesario. Olivia happens to be hanging out of the window and sees this, so she rushes down and drags Sebastian indoors, she also thinking he is Cesario. Sebastian, of course, hasn't a clue who she is, but spots that he is on to a good thing—attractive girl, elegant establishment, masses of servants, etc.—so although astonished when Olivia suggests their getting married, he agrees. A tame priest does the honours and the moment the ceremony is over Sebastian skips off to have a good laugh with Antonio about what has happened.

Things now become even more involved. Orsino, still determined to try and win Olivia, turns up outside her house with Cesario. At the same time, Orsino's aides, who have been chasing about after him with Antonio still in their grip, skid to a halt at the same spot. Antonio, seeing Cesario, thinks she is Sebastian and starts telling Orsino all about their ill-fated voyage in the Adriatic. Orsino, imagining that Antonio is a mental case, humours him by letting him babble on, but he is interrupted by Olivia, who is just coming out of the house to go shopping when she catches sight of Cesario, whom she addresses as 'husband'. Orsino immediately throws a fit, supposing Cesario to have betrayed him, with the woman he loves. Cesario, scared out of her buskins, denies it, of course.

At this moment Olivia's tame priest happens to come along, so she asks him to testify that he has just joined herself and Cesario in wedlock. This the holy man confirms.

With Orsino now at boiling point, Cesario quaking like a jelly, and Olivia in floods, who should come tripping along the street, not a care in the world, but young Sebastian.

32

If thou darest tempt me further, draw thy sword

In a moment all the appalling complexities of the situation become crystal clear. Orsino, being a sensible creature, decides to make the best of a bad job and marry Cesario, who of course is absolutely overjoyed at this unexpected turn-up. Only Malvolio is left out on a limb. He has been locked in a cellar by the servants and is now let out, clutching the letter that led to his undoing and which now turns out to have been written as a joke by Olivia's maid. Absolutely livid, Malvolio stalks off, leaving Olivia's jester to bring the proceedings to a close with the weather report set to music.

Othello

Othello deals with a problem that is unfortunately still with us: the problem of race relations. This is, indeed, a very tricky matter. One knows, or at any rate one has heard, that some of them are perfectly charming, but the thing is, *would you want your daughter to marry one of them?* Some might be inclined to think the situation slightly different in Othello's case because he was a general—not of course in the British army; and not of course that there would have been the slightest prejudice against him in Army circles even if he had been. Anyway, he was in the Venetian army, so they didn't have to worry. Still, his being a general in no way abates the anger of Desdemona's papa, Brabantio, when he hears that she has married Othello secretly. For some unknown reason, this news is conveyed to him in the middle of the night by one Roderigo, who wakes the old man up to give him these tidings. And there and then Brabantio goes rushing off to the Duke of Venice's palazzo to lodge a complaint.

Now, it so happens that the Duke hasn't gone to bed yet, because rumours are flying about of possible enemy action in the Mediterranean. Messengers keep dashing in and out with the latest reports from Intelligence and there is a general atmosphere of crisis. So when poor old Brabantio stumbles into the Cabinet room in his pyjamas and starts gabbling about miscegenation, nobody is inclined to pay much attention to him. But the Duke, being a kindly soul and sorry to see Brabantio in such a state, adjourns a discussion that he is having on naval strategy and gives ear to the old man's complaint.

He then calls on Othello to defend himself against Brabantio's accusations, which include a lot of rot about witchcraft and sorcery and magic potions, and in any case Brabantio is manifestly so prejudiced against all blacks that Othello has no difficulty in persuading one and all that although his skin may be as black as soot, his intentions are as pure as the driven snow. So old Brabantio has to pipe down, though he still feels rather sore.

Othello's GHQ being situated in Cyprus, he now sails

there with Desdemona. On his staff is a bright young officer called Cassio, in whom Othello thinks he has spotted a future military genius. This is resented very deeply by another and slightly older staff officer called Iago, who complains to Roderigo about his being passed over for promotion and about the favouritism shown to Cassio. Incidentally, what on earth Roderigo is doing at GHQ is never explained. He is, after all, a civilian and would appear to have no business to be there at all, except as a convenient receptacle for Iago's bile, and in fact Iago has gone completely round the bend about the matter and never stops going on about the injustice of it all. So deeply has this resentment bitten into his soul that he evolves a fiendish plan to encompass the destruction of Cassio, and, with any luck, Othello too.

By the time they all reach Cyprus the emergency is over; the hostile fleet has been dispersed by a storm and all is quiet. As soon as they arrive, victory celebrations begin, bonfires are lit, fireworks set off and everywhere there is feasting and revelry. This is exactly the chance Iago has been looking for. He plies Cassio with drink until the poor fellow is absolutely pissed and then induces him to pick a quarrel with a perfectly innocent bystander, a character called Montano. Cassio, for no reason, threatens to knock him o'er the mazzard, whereupon Montano says 'You're drunk' and immediately there is a tremendous set-to. Iago whispers to Roderigo to go quickly and ring the alarm bell, so as to wake the whole town, then when the commotion starts, Iago pretends he doesn't know anything about it and wants to know what's up.

In next to no time there is complete chaos. Riot squads are called out, rapiers are flashing all over the stage and the cast is bespattered with tomato ketchup.

Suddenly Othello appears. He asks what the hell is going on. Cassio, who is supposed to be officer of the watch, is too far gone to answer, so Iago, feigning with devilish cunning a reluctance to give the game away, tells Othello how the whole thing started, *ie*, that Cassio in his cups had

What is the matter?

set upon Montano without the slightest provocation and had tried to knock him o'er the mazzard. Result: Cassio has his bars taken away and gets ten days confinement.

Not unnaturally, he is frightfully upset. But Iago, the swine, pretends to make light of it and says not to worry, Othello will soon reinstate him, adding with reptilian guile that his best plan would be to ingratiate himself with Desdemona, who can twist the Moor round her little finger.

Well, truth to tell, Cassio hasn't got very much in the top storey or he wouldn't be taken in for a moment by advice of this sort, which could so very easily lead to trouble—as of course it does. For Iago's next move is to murmur hints into Othello's ear about Cassio and Desdemona, so that when she, having listened sympathetically to Cassio's story, tells her lord and master that she thinks he has given Cassio a raw deal, Othello is just about ready to blow his top. He gets hold of Iago and shakes the daylights out of him—this is where the audience sometimes applauds—and demands proof of his hideous insinuations.

Iago assumes an air of injured innocence—absolutely sickening, he is—but when it comes to villainy he is never at a loss and he has an instant scheme for converting Othello's suspicions into a certainty. He says, do you remember that handkerchief you gave your wife, the one with the strawberries on it? Yes, I remember it, says Othello, what about it? Well, says Iago, the other day I saw Cassio wiping his face with it. Wiping his face? says Othello, on her handkerchief? That's right, says Iago, I saw him. I don't believe it, says Othello. Okay, says Iago, you wait and see. I'll give him wait and see if I catch him with it, Othello says, O blood, blood, blood.

Now, do you know what Iago does? He gets his poor wretched wife, Emilia, who also happens to be Desdemona's maid, to steal the handkerchief while Desdemona is doing the laundry. Then he tells Othello to ask Desdemona what she has done with it. So Othello pretends he has got a splitting headache and asks her to put a drop of *eau de cologne* on a hanky and stick it on his forehead. So she dobs some onto a Kleenex and places it gently on his throbbing noggin, as she supposes it to be, but he says no, he wants the handkerchief with magical properties, meaning the one with the strawberries on it. Poor Desdemona is scared stiff and thinks, oh God, what shall I tell him? She daren't tell him that she has lost it, so she says by way of changing the conversation, 'Seen Cassio lately?' Well, of course, that does it. Othello goes through the roof, exclaiming as he does so, 'Zounds!' So you can tell he is pretty upset.

Well, that night when she goes to bed Desdemona is too tired to read, she just puts the light out and drops straight off.

A little later Othello, who by this time is mad with jealousy, comes upstairs with the idea of doing her in, but she wakes up and wants to know what's going on. So he tells her all about Cassio and the handkerchief and so on, and when she starts to explain he simply won't listen. He gets hold of one of the pillows and smothers the poor girl. But instead of making a proper job of it, he leaves her still breathing.

At this point there is a sudden commotion downstairs and then Emilia outside the bedroom calls out to Othello, 'What ho, my Lord!'—not the sort of remark you would expect from a lady's maid, but still, she's a bit over-excited at this moment and she bounces into the bedroom and tells Othello that Cassio has killed Roderigo. (And this is not just a rumour. What has actually happened is that Iago has put Roderigo up to killing Cassio, only it turned out the other way, Cassio being quicker on the draw.)

Just as Emilia comes in, Desdemona expires. Emilia is rather shocked, not unnaturally, it being perfectly apparent that her death has been caused by foul means. There is a bit of a row and gradually the truth emerges about how Emilia stole the handkerchief and all that, and Othello at last realises that Iago is at the back of it all.

Very conveniently, a lot of strange people come storming into the bedroom just at this moment, and among them is Iago. Othello says that Emilia has told all, whereupon Iago

Away I say ; go out and cry a mutiny

stabs her and makes off, and the others shamble out after him. What they were all supposed to be doing in Desdemona's bedroom at that hour of the night is still a matter of controversy among Shakespearian scholars.

Presently another fellow comes in, a chap called Gratiano, who has already hopped on and off several times, and this silly twit, seeing two dead bodies and Othello prowling about like a tiger, says 'What is the matter?' Othello tells him, and while he is doing so, in no uncertain terms, the rest of them all troop in again, with Cassio in a bath chair, having been rather slashed about in his encounter with Roderigo, and Iago under arrest. Othello promptly stabs Iago and then on second thoughts stabs himself. Whereupon somebody called Ludovico, who is one of those who has been streaming in and out without so much as a by-your-leave, starts telling everybody what to do, and having been given their marching orders, they all troop off and that's the end.

Much Ado About Nothing

The old saying that eavesdroppers seldom hear any good of themselves is given a bit of a twist in *Much Ado*. The corollary seems to be that if they *do* hear anything complimentary, it is a sure sign that something suspicious is going on.

The two leading girls in the play, Hero and Beatrice, are the daughter and niece respectively of Leonarto, the governor of Messina. Hero is ever such a nice girl; in other words, utterly dim, and Beatrice is one of those rather tiresome young women who pride themselves on always speaking their minds. And as the capacity of Beatrice's mind is about equal to that of a goldfish, added to which she always keeps shoving her oar in, she doesn't attract much betting, in spite of her alluring face and figure, in the World's Sweetheart stakes.

One day, three army officers turn up for luncheon at Leonarto's, having been on active service abroad. The three, who are called Benedick, Claudio and Pedro, are old friends of his. Benedick is tremendously full of himself, and Beatrice being the same, there is instant antipathy between them. However, this hardly excuses her saying to him at one point in the conversation, 'I can't think why you bother to go on talking, nobody's listening to a word you're saying'. But Benedick, who is capable of being just as offensive, if rather more subtle, in his remarks, gives as good as he gets.

Leonarto, listening to this exchange of pleasantries, thinks Benedick is frightfully funny, which only makes Beatrice worse. She twits Benedick with being a coward in battle, but as in the recent hostilities he happens to have shown himself to be madly brave, this jibe makes him absolutely fume.

Benedick's friend Pedro, who has also been listening with some amusement to their carry-on, suddenly gets smitten with a very strange idea (not the only one that raises its head in the course of the play). He says to Leonarto (*sotto voce*), 'Wouldn't it be funny if they were to get married?' And the more he thinks about the possibility, the more risible does the whole idea seem to be.

What isn't so funny is that Claudio has meanwhile fallen heavily for Hero, and although to Pedro's way of thinking he might as well get himself hitched to a dead duck, the poor fellow is obviously so dotty about the girl that Pedro decides to put in a good word for him with Leonarto. And Leonarto, never expecting such a dim dull doll as Hero to get away with marriage, gladly agrees to their making a match of it.

Pedro, who is a born mischief-maker, is still bitten with the idea of trying to bring Beatrice and Benedick together, even though oil and water would seem as likely to mix, and he thinks up a scheme such as only Shakespeare could hope to get away with.

Benedick is a bit of an egg-head, and likes nothing better on a hot afternoon than to put his feet up and get his nose stuck into Machiavelli's *Discorsi sulla prima deca di Tito Livio* or something equally entertaining. Pedro waits until he sees Benedick tripping down the garden path with a book, then taking Claudio with him, he goes out into the garden and creeps along under the window of the summer house, where he starts talking in a very loud voice.

He says to Claudio, 'What was that you were saying the other day about Beatie being in love with Benny?' And Claudio, who of course has been put up to it by Pedro, says, 'Oh yes, she's nuts about him. It's just an act, all that pretence of disliking him. She's crazy about him really.'

And there is Benedick sitting in the summer house listening to every word and not knowing whether he is coming or going, because in spite of the way Beatrice treats him, he can't disguise from himself the fact that her face and figure arouse in him something more than distant admiration.

While Benedick is trying to sort himself out, Beatrice suddenly pokes her head through the window and yells out, 'Grub's on'. She follows this lady-like announcement with a few more typically genteel remarks, then she goes back to the house for dinner.

Hero, whom Pedro has also inveigled into his plot, now

By my sword, Beatrice, thou lovest me

takes her turn. She sends one of her maids, a girl called
Margaret, to whom gossip comes as easily as a natural
function, to tell Beatrice that if she pops down to the orchard
she will probably catch Hero talking about her with her
maid.

Beatrice is off down the garden path like a whippet and in
the orchard she sees Hero and her maid Ursula strolling
about under the Granny Smiths, and when they turn round
Beatrice ducks down behind the gooseberries.

As they approach, she listens to them with her eyes
popping, her ears burning and her mouth cram full.

'Don't you ever let on to her about him,' says Hero, 'Poor
soul, she'd rag the life out of him.'

'I know,' says Ursula. 'And to think she hasn't a clue
about what he feels.'

'I think he's rather sweet really,' Hero says. 'And for
shape, for bearing, argument and valour, goes foremost in
report throughout Italy.'

'I beg your pardon?' says Ursula.

'Forget it,' Hero says, and they stroll off, leaving Beatrice
with heaving bosom and severe palpitations.

The result of all this is that the next time B. meets B. they
start cooing at each other like turtle doves, only so far as
Benedick is concerned there is more of the turtle about him
than the dove.

But now malignant fate enters from the prompt corner
in the form of Leonarto's half-brother John, a real bastard
in both senses. His only delight is in upsetting people, and
in Hero's forthcoming marriage to Claudio he sees a
marvellous opportunity for causing the maximum of
annoyance to all parties. He loathes Claudio merely because
Leonarto likes him, and as he loathes Leonarto too, anyone
Leonarto likes is *ipso facto* John's enemy. This bastard gets
hold of another as bad as himself, called Borachio, who
agrees to persuade the girl, Margaret, to dress up in
Hero's clothes and then hang out of the window at midnight—it is the night before Hero's wedding, incidentally—and have a talk with him. Meanwhile, John, the

devil, tells Claudio and Leonarto that he has discovered
Hero is in the habit of chatting up strangers from her
bedroom window in the middle of the night. Of course,
they don't believe a word of it, but all the same he induces
them to have a look for themselves and that night they all
three go along to see if anything will happen, and there is
Margaret pretending to be Hero (a ruse by which Claudio
and Leonarto are completely taken in), hanging out of her
casement and giggling with Borachio.

Claudio, livid, bides his time until the next day, when he
and Hero are actually at the altar, and then he lets her have
it. Tremendous scene, incredulous whistles, tears and
screams, Hero passes out.

A wily old friar now pops up from nowhere in particular
and persuades Leonarto to give it out that Hero, in the
extremity of her grief and shame, has passed away.

'And what on earth good d'you suppose that will do?'
says Leonarto.

The friar says that when Claudio hears that Hero is dead
he will instantly repent of his anger and so when she reap-
pears they will be reconciled—a likely story. But Leonarto
believes it and goes off to give out the sorry tidings.

This leaves Beatrice and Benedick alone, sitting in a pew
discussing the situation.

'If you were half a man,' Beatrice says, 'you'd kill
Claudio.'

'Steady on,' Benedick says, 'after all, he is my best friend,
you know.'

'Suit yourself, it's him or me,' says Beatrice.

Well, after a bit of a struggle with himself Benedick says
he will call Claudio out. But in the meantime Claudio has
been called out by Leonarto—all part of the plan put up
by the old friar. And as Pedro is backing up Claudio, there
they are, all four of 'em, with rapiers drawn and thirsting
for each other's guts, when in marches Dixon of Dock
Green with Borachio, whom he has arrested in the pub,
where the stupid twit has been overheard bragging about
his own nefarious part in the plot.

. . . most wonderful, that she should so dote on Signor Benedick

And so all is brought to light—all, that is, except the friar's little scheme Claudio, still believing Hero to be dead, is awfully cut up and promises to do whatever Leonarto requires of him to make amends. So Leonarto, trying hard not to laugh, insists, for no apparent reason, that Claudio must marry Hero's cousin, a girl he has never even seen. At this point you might think Claudio would smell a rat, but no. All he says is—showing himself to be a man after George Wallace's heart—that he would marry her even 'were she an Ethiope'.

So everything is fixed up and Hero, returning from Beyond the Fringe, turns up at the church wearing a mask and the marriage gets under way, Claudio still totally unsuspecting.

In the middle of the ceremony it suddenly occurs to Benedick, who of course is there more or less as one of the family, that as the occasion seems ripe and the parson is on tap, they might as well make it a double and Beatrice can become his wife at the same time. So they all get married. But not until after they have signed the register does Hero take off her mask, and as the Lambs put it, 'We may be sure that this proved a most agreeable surprise to Claudio.'

As You Like It

The period of this play is that indeterminate era in French history when half the population seemed to be dukes. One, known as Duke Senior, has been usurped and banished from his lands by his younger brother Fred. Senior has become a sort of Errol Flynn, living in the Forest of Arden with a self-supporting community of medieval boy scouts. All are as happy as can be, except Jacques, a walking wet-blanket, but as he only acts as a kind of chorus, we don't hear too much about his woes.

Now when Senior was banished, his only daughter, Rosalind, was prevented from going with him into the unknown by the wicked Fred, whose daughter Celia has no other chum than Rosalind. (Even her best friends won't tell her.)

One Saturday afternoon the two of them go off to see the wrestling—Charles, the king's champion, versus Orlando, an unknown number giving away 28 lbs to his opponent. It looks like a walkover for the champion, and in fact the two girls are so afraid of what he may do to the courageous upstart that they plead with Orlando to call the whole thing off. But the game lad refuses and in the first round, after a bit of give and take, he hoists Charles up in the air and does an airplane spin, then lays him cold with a body-slam followed by a pin-fall. A tremendous scene ensues. Fred is much impressed. He asks the lad his name and is told, 'Orlando, my liege, the youngest son of Sir Rowland de Boys'.

'Ah!' says Fred, 'one of de Boys.'

But he's not joking. The elder de Boys was once a trusted friend of Duke Senior and therefore his very name is anathema to Fred, who stalks off much displeased.

Rosalind feels hideously embarrassed by this and tries to make amends by taking off her beads and putting them round Orlando's neck, so that what with his bobbed hair and bare feet, he only needs some filthy jeans and a pair of dark glasses to pass for a prince of fashion in King's Road, Chelsea.

Orlando thanks her gracefully, adding, 'My better parts

are all thrown down', which isn't surprising after lifting a fellow 28 lbs heavier than himself.

Celia, who makes up for having bad breath by having a sharp eye for the tell-tale minutiae of love, twits her cousin with being stuck on Orlando, which Rosalind freely admits. Little does she know it, but her instant passion is reciprocated in the bosom of Orlando.

Fred, who loves nothing so dearly as a grievance, works himself into a state, thinking about de Boys and Duke Senior and Rosalind being the Duke's daughter and all that, and he makes up his mind to get rid of her. Celia begs and pleads with him, but it is no good. So she decides to go along with Rosalind, who for their better safety dresses up as a man. Being a well set-up sort of girl (and of course bras were unheard of in those days) she has no difficulty, and they go off in the guise of a brother and sister, calling themselves, so as not to attract attention by anything too outlandish, Ganymede and Aliena.

The idea is to find the Duke in the forest, but unfortunately neither of them has the slightest idea where to start looking and after walking for miles they both collapse.

Presently a young shepherd goes by. They ask him where they can find shelter and he says that he knows of a farm that is up for sale. Now Rosalind is no fool. Before leaving, she hid all her savings where she hoped they would be safest, and as Celia, too, has borne away all she could lay hands on, between the two of them they're loaded. So they buy the farm, sight unseen, and move in straight away.

We have to go back a bit here to bring in Orlando's brother Oliver, known as Twist, and rightly. He is supposedly Orlando's guardian, appointed to this office by old de Boys on his death-bed, but he has tried to do Orlando down at every turn. He it was who fixed up the wrestling bout between him and Charles, hoping to be rid of the lad by this cunning stratagem. But having lost a packet through backing the loser, Twist will stop at nothing now, so insensate is his jealousy of the youth's good looks and success with the girls. He decides to have another go at him and

Duke Frederick

roast him to death by setting his bedroom on fire. But an aged individual called Adam, a former minion of de Boys, and now devoted old servant to Orlando, warns his master of what's in the wind and urges him to flee. Knowing the lad hasn't got a bean, owing to the rapacity of Twist, Adam presents Orlando with his life's savings, 125 quid (pathetic, isn't it?) and swears to stick by him. This is no time for sentiment. Orlando, delighted to find himself in funds for the first time in his life, makes off as quickly as he can, old Adam tottering after him as well as his corns, sciatica, bronchial asthma, incontinence and failing sight will allow.

Eventually they fetch up—guess where? In the Forest of Arden! And there Adam has one of his dizzy spells and subsides gently into a bed of stinging nettles, famished for want of the Energen rolls and calve's foot jelly which is about all he can now digest.

Orlando goes off in search of food and by a stroke of good luck falls in with Duke Senior's party, who are having a bite to eat. After explaining to the Duke about old Adam, he is bidden to fetch him to the spot, so he goes to where he has left the aged servitor, picks him up and staggers back to the luncheon party.

Later on, Rosalind and Celia, by another stroke of good luck, happen to bump into Orlando. They have been puzzled by a strange outbreak of vandalism in the forest; someone has been carving Rosalind's name all over the trees. As soon as she sees Orlando, she realises what's up. Now, either Orlando must be so short-sighted as to be a danger to himself and others or so soft in the head as to be ditto. He is completely taken in by Rosalind's get-up, nor does he recognise Celia, who isn't even disguised.

Rosalind spots that Orlando hasn't caught on and being a bit of sport decides to lead him on. She says that she can cure his infatuation by pretending to be his *inamorata*, to whom he shall make love, and she will so abash him by her answers that he'll wish he never even started. Orlando still has enough sense left not to believe in such an idiotic scheme, but for the fun of the thing he agrees to give it a whirl. He makes impassioned love to Ganymede—he/she, of course, is in fits—and each in their own way rather enjoy it.

So far Rosalind hasn't yet run into her father, Duke Senior, but you can see it coming, and when it happens, believe it or not, the old man is as completely taken in by her as Orlando was.

Now, one day Orlando finds a complete stranger lying on the ground being throttled by a snake. Seeing Orlando, the snake unwinds itself and glides away into the undergrowth. But there, couchant and regardant, is a lion proper against a field vert, licking its chops and preparing to carry on where the snake left off. Orlando, cool as marble (though inwardly quaking like a blancmange) draws his sword and runs the beast through, though not before it has given him a very nasty scratch on his arm. At this point the sleeping stranger wakes up and Orlando, to his absolute astonishment, recognises him as Oliver Twist, his long-lost brother. So deeply moved is Twist by Orlando's valour that he instantly repents him of his former wrongs and weeping like a child, begs forgiveness. Orlando, giving him his handkerchief, tells him to stop making such a scene and get up off his knees. All is forgiven and they embrace.

Orlando, still bleeding pretty freely, sends Oliver off to seek first aid, and the first aide he runs into is Rosalind. He explains the situation to her, whereupon she keels over in a dead faint and falls flat on top of him. When she comes to she pretends, of course, that it had absolutely nothing to do with hearing about Orlando's axillary being clawed to shreds but was just the heat.

Oliver goes on with his story, making no attempt whatever to gloss over his past villainies, and so impressed is Celia by his utter and transparent candour that she instantly falls in love with him and consequently he with her, and they decide to get married the next day.

Rosalind now feels it's about time to bring matters to a head, so as soon as she sees Orlando she says to him (speaking, of course, as Ganymede), that if he really does

I am he that is so love-shaked. I pray you tell me your remedy

love Rosalind, he, Ganymede, will cause her to materialise at Celia's wedding, so that subject to the Duke's pleasure, both parties can be married at the same time.

Well, the next day there they all are, waiting to see what is going to happen, most of them sensing an anti-climax. Then Ganymede appears and asks the Duke if he will consent to Rosalind's marriage to Orlando. Nothing to lose, the Duke thinks, so he says yes. Whereupon Rosalind and Celia shoot out of the room and when they come back a few minutes later Rosalind is once more in petticoats. There is a gasp of amazement. All realise in a flash, since they look exactly like each other, that she and Ganymede are one and the same person.

But that is not the end. Just as the nuptials are brought to a close, a messenger arrives from Fred, who had set forth with the idea of capturing and killing the Duke, whose growing popularity had seemed a danger to his own authority. But stalking through the woods, who should he come across but the Rev. Billy Graham—or was it he?— at any rate, some good and holy man under whose moderating influence Fred's wrath against the Duke has been turned to love.

On hearing that his lands and revenues have been restored to him, the Duke is off like a rocket, followed by the whole court, cheering. And so, All's Well That Ends Well, in spite of its being *As You Like It*.

King Lear

The basic problem with which *King Lear* is concerned is one that is as relevant today as it was in Shakespeare's time: what to do if you have got a geriatric relative living in the house. This is the dilemma that faces Lear's three daughters, Goneril, the Duchess of Albany, Regan, the Duchess of Cornwall, and Cordelia, the youngest. She has not yet found a husband, but both the King of France and the Duke of Burgundy are in the running.

Lear, who is over eighty and looks it, decides that the time has come for him to hand over the reins of state to someone younger and more capable than himself; a move which his daughters consider to be long overdue. So he calls the three girls together with the half-baked notion of sharing his kingdom between them in proportion to their deserts, his idea being to try to find out the extent to which each of them loves him.

Now, between ourselves, Goneril and Regan are a pair of downright bitches, devious, calculating and utterly selfish. Cordelia, on the other hand, is an extremely nice girl with absolutely no nonsense about her.

Goneril says to the old man that he is more precious to her than the light of her own eyes, which, if true, would seem to indicate incipient glaucoma. Regan tells him that Goneril is a liar and is only saying what she thinks will please him and that she herself loves him far more dearly. Imagine it, this scrofulous, half-witted old patriarch!

Cordelia, when it is her turn, says that she loves him too, presumably as one might love an old collie that one doesn't quite like to have put down, but that when she marries, Lear will have to do with only half her affection. Well, being accustomed only to the grossest flattery, Lear is livid and cuts Cordelia out of the plan altogether, dividing her portion equally between her brothers-in-law, Albany and Cornwall. But there's a catch in the arrangement. Lear stipulates that he shall stay with each of them in turn for a month at a time for the rest of his life, AND shall be allowed to bring a hundred of his knights with him. Well, of course, not everyone has got that kind of accommodation, let alone the necessities to go with it, or the patience to put up with such a mob appearing every other month.

Cordelia is naturally very distressed about the whole thing, especially as Lear tells her off in front of the entire court, which is fearfully embarrassing. No one knows quite where to look or what to say, except the Earl of Kent. The Earl has always been tremendously loyal, so when he sees Lear making such a complete ass of himself he deems it best to try to bring him to his senses with a few home truths. But his words have just the opposite effect. Lear has to be practically tied down. He banishes Kent instantly; that is to say, he gives him till the end of the week to get out.

Then he calls in France and Burgundy and says what about it? Well, as soon as Burgundy hears that Cordelia has been disinherited, you can't see his heels for dust, but France sticks by his word and says he'll make her Queen of France. Before she goes down to catch the boat, she begs Goneril and Regan to look after old Lear, still having some feelings of affection for the poor old dotard, but they tell her in no uncertain terms to mind her own business.

And now Lear begins to realise what's what. Long before his month at Goneril's place is up, she makes it painfully obvious that the best thing he and his hundred knights can do is go and get stuffed. Moreover, she tells the servants not to answer the bell if he rings, nor to do a hand's turn for any of his unfortunate retinue, and then she has the gall to complain to Lear about them all and their riotous behaviour, which is absoloutely untrue, because a more saintly collection of knights bachelor you couldn't find in a month of Methodist Sundays.

In the meantime, the devoted Kent puts on a pair of false whiskers and, calling himself Caius, tries to get a job on Lear's staff. It shows how far gone the old man is when it becomes apparent that he is completely taken in by this infantile manoeuvre and in next to no time the so-called Caius is once more an indispensable member of Lear's household.

Another who sticks by the old man is his Fool, a profes-

Goneril, Regan and Cordelia

sional gag-man, whose wit is of the same kind as the wit of that pathetic fallacy known as an Arkansas comedian.

Now Goneril has got a steward called Oswald, a thoroughly uncouth twit, who starts making fun of old Lear, whereupon Caius trips him up and he lands on his behind. Lear is delighted, this being just the sort of thing he enjoys. But not unnaturally, he is mortified beyond words by Goneril's treatment of him and he decides to go and stay with the Cornwalls instead. So he writes a note to Regan saying that he and the knights will be over at about tea-time and sends Caius round with it. But Goneril is a jump ahead. She has already dispatched the egregious Oswald to Regan with a letter of her own, telling a pack of lies about the old man. And thus when Caius gets there, the first thing he espies through the peep-hole of the postern gate is Oswald's greasy visage, grinning triumphantly. They immediately start scrapping and before you can say Jack the Robinson, Oswald is out for the count. In a matter of moments Caius finds himself in the stocks, and that is where Lear finds him when he turns up for the cucumber sandwiches and lapsang suchong.

To Lear's rage and embarrassment, he soon finds out that things are a jolly sight worse at Regan's than they were even at Goneril's. Regan tells him flatly that she is prepared to put up with twenty-five of his wretched old knights, but won't have one more. Lear, who has always been surrounded by a sycophantic mob, morning, noon and night, simply can't imagine himself with hardly more than two dozen of the lads around him. So he swallows what's left of his pride, poor old duffer, and shambles back to Goneril, only to find that she has now changed her mind and won't have any knights at all on the premises. If he wants to stay, she says, he will have to rely on her own domestic staff. But to Lear, who, after all, has been a monarch of sorts, this is more than flesh and blue blood will stand. He calls the girls a pair of unnatural hags (understatement of the week) and storms out of the house in the middle of the night.

And what a night it is! Blowing a full gale and raining

cats and dogs. The back-stage staff don't know whether they're coming or going, thunder rolling, lightning flashing and wind-machine going full pelt. And on top of everything else, the Fool (and who but a complete idiot would venture out on such a night?) starts singing a topical number about the wind and the rain.

Well, by great good fortune, Kent comes across them— (and what, you may ask, is *he* doing out in such a night? The answer is, he is keeping the plot boiling)—and he leads them to the shelter of an absolutely disgusting hovel occupied by a mentally deranged person, whom Lear starts upbraiding for no reason at all, except that by this time he is even further out of his wits than usual.

Daybreak sees the wretched trio tramping towards Dover, from which point Kent hops over to France to find Cordelia and tell her what has been happening. She persuades the King, her husband, to send her to England with an army. And lo and behold, what is the first thing they see on arriving at Dover, but Lear walking about on the sea-front wearing a picture-hat trimmed with flowers and talking to himself, from which Cordelia draws the inference that all is not well with the old boy. However, to cut a long story short, she eventually nurses him back to his senses—no mean task—and there for the moment we must leave them both.

Meanwhile, the two ugly sisters have got themselves involved as rivals with a bastard called Edmund, who, by devious manoeuvres that would have done credit to a Caribbean politician, has made himself Earl of Gloucester. Regan's husband having died (and who could blame him?) she announces that she and Gloucester are to be wed forthwith. The jealous Goneril, however, has a brilliant idea for preventing this: she poisons Regan. But Albany, learning for the first time of Goneril's passion for Glouces- ter, claps her into prison, where she commits suicide.

Now, what of Cordelia? Well, she, poor girl, is captured and imprisoned by Gloucester, and unable to withstand the penal conditions of the period, she languishes and dies.

Ay, every inch a king

The faithful Kent reveals his identity to Lear, but by this time Lear can't take anything in and hasn't the faintest idea what's going on, which isn't surprising, as a matter of fact, as at this point the story is a bit difficult to follow. Anyway, he dies too, leaving Kent, Albany and Edgar (Edgar? Who on earth is Edgar?) to make their exit to the strains of a funeral march.

All's Well That Ends Well

It must be admitted that there are elements of improbability in a good many of Shakespeare's plots and *All's Well That Ends Well* is no exception. But let us begin at the beginning.

Bertram, Count of Rousillon, has had an invitation to go and stay with the King of France, a former friend of Bertie's dead father. A funny old man called Lafeu has been sent by the King to escort Bertie to Paris, a very civil gesture, considering that Bertie is perfectly capable of going to Paris by himself. Old Lafeu is having a chat with Bertie's mother, the Countess, before they take off and the subject of the King's health crops up. It turns out that the King has got a fistula, not a malady that is usually referred to in polite society, but as the Countess hasn't a clue about where a fistula usually gets you, she is none the wiser.

The Countess has a paid companion, a girl called Helena, whose father was a very well known GP, Dr Gerard de Narbon. The Countess says what a pity it is that he is not alive, as he probably could have cured the King. As a matter of fact, he has only just died and at the mention of him Helena suddenly bursts into floods. But in fact she is not lamenting her father, as they fondly imagine, she is lamenting Bertie's imminent departure. The trouble with Helena is that she has the most frightful inferiority complex and although she is dotty about Bertie, she is convinced there is no future in it because of her lowly social status. She has neither rank nor wealth, and in fact all she possesses is a lot of her father's old prescriptions.

After Bertie has been away for a little while, the Countess's butler, who has a nose like a gun-dog for the least breath of scandal, tells her that he has heard Helena talking to herself about Bertie and about clearing out and going to Paris to look for him.

Later on, the Countess taxes Helena with this and in fear and trembling in case she gets the sack, Helena admits that what the butler heard is true. She explains that what put the idea into her head was the discovery among her father's prescriptions of a cure for fistula and that if she can get the King to try it and it works, then obviously the sky's the limit—she will be made. (She hasn't, incidentally, been made up to till now. She is still a virgin and acutely conscious of the fact, as she tells one of Bertie's friends in confidence.)

The Countess, who is extremely fond of Helena and would be quite glad to see her settle down at Rousillon with Bertie, sends her to Paris at her own expense. When she gets there Helena goes to see old Lafeu and through him gets an audience with the King. Well, the long and the short of it is that the King says he will give the prescription a try. In fact, he'll try anything at the moment because he can't even sit down, and that's not the worst of it. However, he makes one condition: if he isn't cured within two days, Helena shall be executed. If the remedy works, then she can choose whichever of the King's courtiers she likes as a husband. Fair enough, says Helena, which is a pretty good indication of her confidence in the remedy; either that or a clear sign that she has lost her reason.

Well, believe it or not, after two days the King *is* cured. He can actually sit down again, and so doing, with Helena at his side, he orders a youthful parcel of noble bachelors to be brought in for her to choose from. Needless to say, the parcel includes Bertie and she chooses him. But Bertie has other ideas. He has always liked Helena, but not in that way, and in any case, as he says, 'A poor physician's daughter my wife? Disdain rather corrupt me ever.' In other words, he is a crashing snob and it is only under pressure from the King that he consents to go through with it.

Now, no sooner are they married than he gets leave from the King to go abroad, and meanwhile sends Helena back to his mother without even saying goodbye to her. What is worse is that as soon as she arrives at Rousillon she gets a long letter from Bertie saying it is all over between them and he hasn't the slightest intention of returning to her; at least, not unless she can get hold of a ring that he always wears on his finger, 'which never shall come off'. Of course, only a cad would try to make a joke out of it.

Count Bertram

The next morning Helena is nowhere to be found and then the butler brings the Countess a note from her saying that she has decided to go on a pilgrimage to Italy, or more precisely to Florence, where by a strange coincidence Bertie is strutting about, having got a commission in the Duke of Florence's army, otherwise known as *esèrcito di Papà* or Dad's Army.

Helena settles down in a boarding house run by a rather nice woman, a widow, who has a daughter of about Helena's age, called Diana. On the evening that Helena arrives they take her off to the Military Tournament, and there is Bertie showing off like mad. The story of his marriage already seems to be common property. The widow, little suspecting to whom she is talking, repeats the story to Helena with some disgust, as Bertie is now chasing Diana, who, coming from a respectable middle-class Italian family, flatly refuses to yield herself to him, even though she finds him by no means unattractive. As a matter of fact, Bertie has been trying to get Diana to let him climb into her bedroom that very night, because he is leaving Florence the next morning.

A plan instantly formulates itself in Helena's mind. She tells Diana and her mother who she is—both of them are of course amazed—and persuades the mother to pretend to allow Diana to arrange an assignation with Bertie. So Diana gets hold of him and says that as it is his last night in Florence, she is willing to lower the drawbridge.

What goes on in her bedroom that night is nobody's business. Of course, the joke is that Helena, having fixed things with Diana, is standing in—or rather, lying in—for her, but as it is pitch dark Bertie can't see a thing and is so unbelievably idiotic that he hasn't the faintest idea that the little lady by his side is not Diana, but Helena.

Before they part, not only has this half-wit promised to marry her, but in token of his vow has given her the ring off his finger, the one he said would never come off—inwardly Helena is laughing like a drain at this point—and in return she gives him one that the King gave her in part-payment of

What I can do can do not hurt to try

her fee, it being an understood thing between them that she would never part with it except to send it back to the old boy if she were ever in dire distress. So you can see what is going to happen a mile off.

At this point you can also see the sort of complications that are starting to build up, and they are going to get far worse. Bertie goes back to the French court sporting Helena's ring. The King immediately spots it and jumps to the conclusion that she has been murdered by Bertie, who, instead of telling the truth (which, of course, would undo the plot and bring the play to a premature end) tells a cock-and-bull story about some woman having thrown it at him out of a window. The King is not such a fool as he looks, fortunately: he doesn't believe a word of the story and in next to no time Bertie finds himself in the hands of the Sûreté.

And now, without a word of explanation, Diana and her mother suddenly turn up. However, the reason for their appearance soon becomes clear. They want the King to compel Bertie to take Diana as his wife, alleging that he promised to make an honest woman of her after they had spent a night together. Bertie flatly denies this, of course, then Diana fishes Helena's ring out of her bag (which Helena has given her) and says that on the night in question she and Bertie exchanged rings during a brief interlude for rest and refreshment.

The King sees that the whole thing is a pack of lies and tells them both, Bertie and Diana, that unless they tell the truth immediately, it's the axe for both of them. 'You boggle shrewdly,' he says to Bertie, which is no exaggeration.

Diana then changes her story and says that the ring was actually given to her by a jeweller and she asks to be allowed to send for him to give evidence. Everybody expects to see some little man with an attaché case and glasses, but instead Helena comes in, obviously in an interesting condition. She explains the whole thing, whereupon Bertie, having been trying to lay Diana for months, switches his affections there and then to Helena. You would think she might have enough sense to realise what an unmitigated swine he is, but no. On the contrary, she is delighted, no doubt seeing herself already as the Countess of Rousillon.

This leaves Diana rather out on a limb, so the King says to her, 'If thou beest yet a fresh uncropped flower,' which is rather a nice way of putting it, 'choose thou thy husband, and I'll pay thy dower,' which is more then generous, seeing that she hasn't the slightest claim on him and that they have only known each other for about ten minutes. So for both girls it turns out to be a case of As You Like It, although in fact it happens to be *All's Well That Ends Well*.

Hamlet

In *Hamlet* an unfortunate situation is seen to exist almost from the moment the curtain goes up. Hamlet's mother, Gertrude, Queen of Denmark, who is a thoroughly unpleasant woman, has recently lost her husband. Or rather, she has lost one and found another in the shape of her brother-in-law, Claudius. Hamlet doesn't like his shape or his looks, and also thinks it is extremely bad form for his mother to have married again so soon after his father's death. So rather ostentatiously he goes on wearing full court mourning long after everyone else is back in bright colours.

One evening, Hamlet is hanging about on the battlements with some friends, none of them having much to do, when a ghost comes along. It turns out to be Hamlet's father. They have a chat, the ghost and Hamlet, and presently the ghost explains that he didn't die from a snake-bite, which was certified as being the cause of death, but was murdered by his loving brother Claudius.

Now, Hamlet had a pretty shrewd suspicion that something of this sort had happened, so he isn't awfully surprised. He is very annoyed, though, and decides to get even with his uncle somehow or other. Just to put him off his guard, Hamlet pretends that grief for the loss of his old man has sent him partly round the bend, which Claudius, who has always thought Hamlet a bit cracked, has no difficulty in believing.

One day a repertory company turns up at the castle and puts on a show that gives Hamlet rather a good idea. He arranges for the cast to do a play that he has written called *The Mousetrap*, which they give at a command performance. In the play, one of the characters, who has designs on the wife and property of another character, poisons him by putting some horrible muck in his ear. This being exactly what Claudius has done, from similar motives, it is a bit too near the knuckle for him, and in the middle of the performance he gets up and totters outside. Later on, as an excuse, a courtier is told to put it about that the dirty dog has been taken ill, suffering from distemper.

Rosencrantz and Guildenstern

Gertrude sends for Hamlet to come and see her in her bedroom, in order to tick him off because of his uncivil behaviour towards herself and the King. In actual fact, Claudius has put her up to this, not knowing exactly how much Hamlet has found out about his operations and hoping that he may reveal himself if he thinks he is alone with his Ma. The King has also ordered a courtier called Polonius (who is really a bit gaga, poor old soul) to hide behind the bedroom curtains and listen to the conversation. Polonius, by the way, despite his advancing years, is not altogether past it and has quite a charming young daughter called Ophelia, who is unofficially engaged to Hamlet.

Inevitably a row develops between Hamlet and his mother and some harsh words are said. Eventually there are actual fisticuffs and Gertrude starts shouting. Poor old Polonius, who can't see a thing behind the curtains and can only hear what is going on, fears the worst and squeaks out at the top of his lungs, 'What ho, help, help, help'. Hamlet, mistaking his voice for the King's (he really needs a hearing aid, poor boy), lunges at the curtain with his sword, which penetrates Polonius in the midriff and the old thing sinks to the ground remarking, 'O I am slain', which is perfectly true.

The King cannot very well overlook this breach of court etiquette by Hamlet, but on the other hand, Hamlet is tremendously popular with the great Danish public, so the King is a bit nervous about doing anything too drastic. However, it is typical of his devious mind that eventually he decides to get rid of Hamlet by sending him abroad—to England, in fact—in the care of two frightful swine called Rosencrantz and Guildenstern Ltd. The King secretly gives them a letter to present to some fellow at the English court asking him to see to it that as soon as Hamlet lands at Felixstowe he shall be given the works and chalked up as missing.

But Hamlet, knowing how Claudius's mind works, suspects there is something of this sort in the wind and on the night ferry somewhere between the Kattegat and the

Skagerrak he manages to get hold of this letter which the King has written. In spite of appearances, Hamlet has a very good sense of humour and he unseals the letter and rubs out his own name and puts in Rosencrantz and Guildenstern's names instead. Then he seals the letter up again and puts it back in their cabin.

Soon after this, the ship is attacked by pirates. They capture Hamlet, but the others escape and the ship sails on to England, with Messrs Rosencrantz and Guildenstern blissfully unaware of what is in store for them, while Hamlet aboard the pirate brigantine is laughing his head off.

He is no use to the pirates (he is not much use to anyone, come to that—far too moody and introspective; not for nothing is he known at court as 'a slice of Danish Blue')—so the pirates put him ashore not far from home, and he turns up again at the castle just in time for Ophelia's funeral. Poor girl, she fell into the river while out botanizing, and apparently being unable to swim, she drownded.

A rather unfortunate incident now occurs. Ophelia's brother, a youth called Laertes, sees Hamlet not only as the murderer of his father, but also as being morally responsible for Ophelia's death through his indifference towards her, because of which she committed suicide. That, at least, is Laertes' theory, and when he spots Hamlet in the crowd at the graveside, he goes for him in front of everybody. In fact, they have a real set-to and at one point they are actually clobbering each other on top of the coffin, a foretaste of *comédie noire*.

Their having been so livid with each other (though later on they shake hands) gives Claudius a marvellous chance to manoeuvre Hamlet up the creek. He gets Laertes to challenge Hamlet to a fencing match, although Hamlet is an épée champion. The whole court crowds into the drawing room to watch the match and some of the courtiers start taking bets on the side. Claudius, two-faced villain that he is—both of them are equally repulsive—eggs Hamlet on and even drinks his health in a mug of Neirsteiner. The filthy fact is that he has bribed Laertes to smear the tip

Thou mixture rank, of midnight weeds collected
With Hecate's ban thrice blasted, thrice infected

of his foil with some sort of deadly poison, so when Hamlet gets pinked in the bicep, Laertes and the King exchange devilish glances. This looks like the *coup de grâce*, and so it is—for Laertes, the dirty traitor, as well as for Hamlet, because when Laertes turns aside to wink at Claudius, he accidentally drops his foil, and Hamlet snatches it up and sticks it into him.

At this point Gertrude suddenly lets out a piercing scream. She has been going at a noggin of Niersteiner too, but she has picked the wrong one. In case the poisoned foil dodge didn't come off, Claudius had prepared a stoup of wine with just a squeeze of hemlock in it, which he was going to offer to Hamlet if Laertes failed to polish him off. But now poor old Gertrude has quaffed it instead and is writhing all over the stage like a squib. At this point, Laertes, realising he has had it, tells Hamlet what he has done, but says the King put him up to it. So then Hamlet runs Claudius through the gizzard and there they are, all four of them, either dead or dying. Hamlet has earlier remarked, 'To be, or not to be, that is the question—' and now he knows the answer.

Measure for Measure

The setting of this play is the gay city of Vienna, where under the linden trees the gay Viennese have been stuffing cream cakes for generations, with the result that they have all become utterly demoralized and Vienna is now known as one of the most dissolute and enjoyable cities in Europe.

Its duke, Vincentio, a man of slow wits, at last becomes aware of what is going on. For instance, according to the law, any man who goes to bed with a woman not his wife is liable to execution, but naturally nobody has paid the slightest attention to this for ages and things have gone on just as they do anywhere else.

Vincentio, dimly aware that all this may eventually lead to a total collapse of morals in the gay city, decides to put the brake on. But he hasn't the guts to do it himself, knowing where he would end up if he tried to. So he shoves it on to his deputy, an egregious worm called Angelo, and gives it out that he himself is going off for a week or two to Poland.

Now, the thing is that Vincentio doesn't altogether trust Angelo (he may be dumb, poor old Vince, but he's not as dumb as all that), so instead of going away, he dresses up as a clergyman and hangs about to see how Angelo is going to deal with the situation.

The first thing Angelo does is to pounce on an unfortunate youth called Claudio, who, like the rest of them, has been having an affair, in this case with a nice little thing called Juliet. Despite the intervention of Escalus, an ancient courtier and a friend of Claudio's father, Angelo orders Claudio to be beheaded.

While he is sitting miserably in the condemned cell, cursing his fate and Angelo, Claudio is visited by a friend called Lucio. He says to Lucio, 'Look, for God's sake go and tell Isabella' (she is Claudio's sister) 'to get on to Angelo and see what she can do.' Not a very hopeful proposition, as Isabella is about to take the veil and all that goes with it.

However, Lucio goes round to the convent where Isabella is immured and yells out to her. But she is deep in converse with one of the nuns and at first she doesn't answer, it being against the rules for a nun to speak to one of the opposite sex (excuse the expression). But the nun isn't a bad old sort and no doubt remembering the days when she too could behave like a human being, she tells Isabella to answer Lucio. So she does.

'Who's that which calls?' she says, not having much regard for syntax.

To which Lucio replies, 'Hail virgin, if you be, as those cheek-roses proclaim you are no less', a sentence fraught with all manner of ambiguities and arguable assumptions. When he tells Isabella what has happened to poor Claudio, she agrees to go and plead with Angelo. In fact, when she gets to his house she crawls round the floor after him, clutching his dressing gown and begging him to impose a suspended sentence on Claudio instead of giving him the chop.

He refuses to listen, but she goes on and on at him till he can't stand it any longer; so eventually he says he'll think about it and tells her to come back the next day.

Now, one remark of Isabella's has stuck in Angelo's nasty little mind: 'Is your own conscience perfectly clear?' Well, of course, it isn't, and furthermore, Isabella, who is absolutely ravishing to look at, has put all sorts of ideas into Angelo's head. The obvious one won't be denied. In fact, he can think of nothing else, and the next day when Isabella comes round he unfolds his sordid plan: her virginity in exchange for Claudio's life.

Isabella is so innocent, poor girl, that at first she thinks he is having her on, though in the circumstances it seems a joke in rather poor taste. When she realises he is in earnest, she is furious and threatens to expose him. Angelo, very nonchalant, asks her whom will the world more readily believe, she with her accusation or him with his denial? Well, of course, she knows the answer, poor thing, and she departs in tears.

Meanwhile, Vincentio has got himself a job as the prison chaplain, and seeing where his little scheme has landed

Must he needs die?

Claudio, he feels a bit guilty about it and tries to give him comfort, though it is hard to think what you can say to cheer up a body that is about to be severed from its head.

Not to keep poor Claudio in suspense, Isabella hies her to the prison and there a rather undignified argument takes place. She having told Claudio about Angelo's proposal, his answer is, 'So what?' He cannot understand her reluctance to save his head, nor she his indifference to what it would cost her.

In the middle of their argument the Reverend Vincentio walks in. 'Sorry,' he says, 'couldn't help overhearing what you were saying' (he had been standing there for ten minutes with his ear glued to the keyhole) 'and it's all right. At least, for Isabella. Angelo was only trying to test her virtue. But he's still got it in for you, old lad, so if I were you I'd get down on your knees. That's how they'll want you tomorrow morning anyway.' And poor old Claudio creeps off, feeling very hard done by.

But in fact, Vincentio has thought of a crafty plan to save Claudio. It turns out that Angelo is a married man. This Vincentio has discovered from Angelo's wife, Mariana (they are separated, by the way), with whom he has ingratiated himself in the role of vicar—you can just imagine the type, can't you? Mariana has told him the full story of their unhappy married life. Everything was all right until she went on a cruise with her brother, in the course of which the yacht in which they were sailing sank, and so did her brother *and* her bank balance. Whereupon, Angelo faked an excuse for leaving her, making out that she had been having it off on the side with somebody else. Needless to say, there was not a word of truth in this, Mariana being known far and wide to be whiter than a pair of old socks washed in Ivory Snow.

For some obscure reason she still feels attached to Angelo, and so falls in at once with Vincentio's scheme, which seems to offer some hope of reconciliation between her and her infamous lord.

The idea is that Isabella shall tell Angelo that on second

thoughts she will agree to his bargain and yield herself. (In fact, it will, of course, be Mariana who turns up.) The assignation is to be at midnight in the back garden, because there it is dark, and so Angelo, supposedly, won't know one from t'other.

All goes well and Mariana gets off to a good start. Meanwhile, Vincentio, knowing Angelo to be as crooked as a corkscrew, decides to go along to the prison to make sure that Claudio's life really will be spared. And it is just as well that he does so, because when he gets there he finds that Angelo, the scheming rat, has given orders for the execution to be advanced and that Claudio's head is to be brought to him next morning with his breakfast.

Well, when put to it, Vincentio can charm the birds off the trees and he has no difficulty in persuading the prison governor, a half-witted retired major, to send Angelo some-body else's head (Angelo, never having seen Claudio, won't know the difference), so they go down to the mortuary and rootle round till they find the noggin of a likely-looking lad and send it over.

This done, Vincentio, in his own name, writes a letter to Angelo, saying that he really can't face Poland, so he's on his way home. At the same time, he tells Angelo to meet him at the entrance to the city the next day and to announce publicly that anyone who has got a complaint to make and wants to present a petition about it should be there too. (They had not yet stumbled on the idea of an ombudsman to look into their grievances with that sense of urgency, that relentless vigour, and that keen and persistent curiosity that characterise the office in our own time.)

Early in the morning Isabella goes along to the prison, having arranged to meet Vincentio there, and he, for reasons of his own, tells her that Claudio has been axed. She gets rather upset at this news, so the wily cleric, to calm her down, tells her that when the Duke returns to the city later in the day, she should lodge a complaint against Angelo on the grounds of seduction and malfeasance. He then slinks off to see Lady Angelo, and they hatch a little plan.

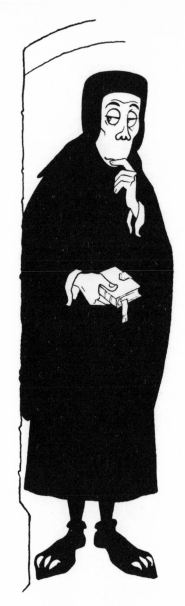

Duke Vincentio

Vincentio's next move is to race out of the city, change into his ducal gear, and then come sauntering back again, to be received on the outskirts by the fawning Angelo and half the populace scrabbling to present petitions.

From this mob, Vincentio—or the Duke, as we must now call him—picks out Isabella, who, conveniently failing to recognise him without his dog-collar, repeats the story he has told her to tell. But in the middle of it, Mariana Angelo pipes up and says there isn't a word of truth in it. She reveals herself as Angelo's wife (while he stands grinding his teeth in the background) and says that at the time Isabella claims she was with him, she herself and Angelo were together in the potting shed.

This Isabella denies. 'Ask the Reverend Lodowick,' (which was the name Vincentio adopted for his pose as a parson), 'he knows the truth'.

But as by this time it is impossible to know who on earth to believe, Angelo asks the Duke to let him and old Escalus find out what it's all about, thus putting himself in the position of both judge and jury. The Duke agrees and says that in the meantime he will withdraw. Which means, of course, that as soon as he is outside the door, he scurries away and dresses up as a parson again, and then comes back to give evidence.

'Where's the Duke?' he says. 'He should hear me speak.'

'You'll speak to him through us or not at all,' says Escalus, 'so watch it.'

Well, first of all, Lodowick, so-called, blames the Duke for leaving Isabella's case in the hands of Angelo, since he is the one she has accused. Old Escalus, furious at hearing the Duke criticized, tells him to shut up, or 'We'll touse you joint by joint,' he says. But Lodowick goes boldly on and says that gay Vienna has become a moral cesspit (are you there, Mrs Mary Whitehouse?) and then attacks Escalus for trying to stop him telling the truth.

At this point—and not a moment too soon—a great transformation scene occurs. Lodowick throws off his disguise, to the horror, joy, astonishment, mystification or what you will, according to whether you are Angelo, Escalus, Mariana, Lucio, Juliet, Isabella, Mrs Whitehouse, or the populace.

He reveals that Claudio is still alive, and pardons him on condition that he marries Juliet. At first, he refuses to pardon Angelo, then Mariana, kneeling before him, pleads for her lord's life. Hoping to tip the balance, she says to Isabella, 'Lend me your knees', and that does it. The Duke is doubled up. Angelo is pardoned too, and then—as if you didn't know it—the Duke claims Isabella for his lawful wedded wife.

A Midsummer Night's Dream

The hideous complexities of *The Dream*, as it is called by those who want to show their intimate knowledge of the theatrical profession, would almost justify one in calling this play A Midsummer Night's Nightmare. Basically, it concerns a series of misunderstandings—between an engaged couple, Hermia and Lysander, a disengaged couple, Helena and Demetrius, and a rather quarrelsome pair, Titania and Oberon, who are married. These last two are fairies; at least he is, or is often played as one. And on the sidelines, among a horde of other characters, is Theseus, Duke of Athens (where it is all supposed to take place), and a collection of rustics with such well-known Athenian names as Bottom, Snug, Snout, etc. There is also Puck, who is Oberon's side-kick, a naughty little elf with pointed ears and an extremely elementary sense of humour.

The situation, if you can follow it, is this: under Athenian law (and it is probably the same under the Colonels as it was then), death is the penalty for any girl who refuses to marry the husband of her father's choice. Hermia's father, Egeus, has ordered her to marry Demetrius, but it's just not on. She loves Lysander, and in any case her best friend, Helena, is in love with Demetrius (though he, unfortunately, has rather gone off her and is now in love with Hermia). So at Lysander's suggestion Hermia agrees to meet him in a wood and then go to his aunt's house in the suburbs, which are outside the jurisdiction of Athens proper, and there they will get married.

Knowing Helena as she does, Hermia ought to realise that it will be madness to breathe a word of all this to her, but you know what girls are like, she can't resist telling her, and of course Helena, in whom there is a strong streak of masochism, at once goes and tells Demetrius, knowing full well that he will rush off to the wood and try to intercept Helena and Lysander.

We now have to switch to Oberon and Titania. He has got his eye on a small boy, a young Indian, whom Titania has kidnapped, and whom he fancies as a page, but Titania flatly refuses to give the child up. Oberon is frightfully

81

I do but beg a little changeling boy

irritated about this and decides to pay her out. He sends
Puck off to find a special flower, the juice of which, when
applied to the optic nerve, has the curious property of
reducing one's powers of social discrimination virtually to
nil and at the same time triggers off an instantaneous sexual
urge. So that if applied, for instance, while one is asleep,
the first living thing that is seen on waking up becomes an
object of love. Oberon's hope is, of course, that by administering the drug to Titania he shall cause her to make an
exhibition of herself by proclaiming her love for some
totally inappropriate object, for instance, a bear, a wolf, or
possibly a chimpanzee, if there should happen to be one
knocking about on the outskirts of Athens.

While he is waiting in the wood for Puck, Oberon sees
Helena trailing along after Demetrius, moaning about the
switch in his affections. So when Puck returns, Oberon,
who is sorry to see Helena in the dumps, tells him to go
after them and squeeze a bit of the magical juice into the
eyes of Demetrius, so that when he catches sight of Helena,
providing he doesn't see someone else first, he will be all
over her again.

Now, the first person Puck sees in the wood is not
Demetrius, but Lysander, who is asleep, and the silly little
ass, instead of going back to Oberon to verify his instructions, squirts the stuff at Lysander, and as luck will have it,
the first person *he* claps eyes on when he wakes up is Helena.

Meanwhile, Oberon, walking through the wood, comes
upon Titania. There on a bank where the wild thyme blows,
his wife is stretched out having a doze. Seeing this, he takes
the opportunity to squirt *her* in the eye.

But that is not the end of it. Oberon finds out that Puck
has dealt with Lysander by mistake instead of Demetrius,
so he goes dashing about the wood till he finds Demetrius
still asleep and squirts him in the eye as well. When
Demetrius wakes up the first person *he* claps eyes on is also
Helena, so now both he and Lysander are chasing after the
same girl. Naturally, she thinks they are both kidding and
she is furious, as they are with each other, and Hermia is

83

furious, too, because of Lysander ditching her for a girl she has always thought was her best friend.

Meanwhile, Bottom, one of the Athenian yokels, has gone out for a walk in the wood—and there must be something about the place, because as soon as anybody sets foot in it they lie down and go sound asleep. Bottom and Titania are both kipping near the same spot and Oberon, seeing this, thinks he'll have a bit of fun. Very conveniently, some ass has left an ass's head lying about, presumably a prop used in some rustic revels or sylvan masque, and Oberon, without waking Bottom, slips it over his head. It is plain to see that Bottom is a fairly simple type, but it rather stretches one's credulity to imagine that he is so simple as to be completely unconscious of the fact that he is wearing a papier-maché mask as big as a coal scuttle and covered with fur. But be that as it may, Titania, when she wakes, sees Bottom and is enraptured.

Oberon teases her about making such a fool of herself, which she has to admit, then he raises the question again of this wretched little Indian boy. He is really quite shameless in his desire to get hold of the dusky little lad and eventually Titania says, oh well, all right, and so Oberon gives her some sort of antidote for the love philtre and she recovers straight away. An interesting side-effect of the antidote is that, having spent years quarrelling with each other like cat and dog, they suddenly become completely reconciled, though how long the reconciliation will last is anybody's guess.

Together they tramp off through the wood to look for Helena and the others, and find that Puck has inveigled them all to the same spot, and there they are, all four of them dead to the world. Oberon applies his antidote to Lysander's eyes and then they all wake up, a little stiff and damp no doubt, but once more in their right minds and affections.

There is still a problem for Hermia though, and what she should do about her situation. Should she marry Lysander and risk the possibility of being cut off in her

Is all our company here?

prime with an axe, or should she kowtow to her horrid old father and marry Demetrius, knowing that he is stuck on Helena? The problem is solved very neatly by the totally unexpected appearance of her father, who is ranging through the wood, looking for her. When he hears that Demetrius hasn't the slightest intention of marrying her, he feels a bit small. Of course, it's his own fault for having been so insistent in the first place without bothering to find out what Demetrius's feelings were. Anyway, he tries to put as good a face on it as he can and they all troop off to see a panto given by the rustics, after which the fairies do a ballet and the curtain comes down to the strains of Mendelssohn.

Romeo and Juliet

As Shakespeare himself remarked, 'the course of true love never did run smooth'. It is in the previous play, *A Midsummer Night's Dream*, that this incontrovertible maxim occurs, not, as you might suppose, in *Romeo and Juliet*, applied to which it seems something of an under-statement.

It all began, you see, with this dance given by Lady Capulet for her daughter Juliet. Practically everybody in Verona had been asked, except the Montagues, because the Capulets and the Montagues were not on speaking terms. As a matter of fact, they hadn't been for ages and the only remarks exchanged between them for some years would still have been unprintable in the days before it became fashionable to lard one's conversation with obscenities.

Notwithstanding this estrangement between Montagues and Capulets, Lord Montague's son, the Honourable Romeo Montague, has agreed to a suggestion by his cousin Benvolio that it might be rather a lark to try and gate-crash Lady Capulet's party. In order to avoid any possibility of detection Romeo decides to wear a mask. This ingenious ruse works a treat. Although, as he is one of the leaders of the *jeunesse dorée* of Verona, his appearance is well-known to practically everyone at the party, not a soul recognizes him.

During the evening he gets off with a rather angelic-looking girl, but being extremely ingenuous, in spite of a certain air of sophistication, he fails at first to realise who she is and is thunderstruck when he later discovers that she is the belle of the ball, Juliet Capulet. But by this time she has disappeared.

Throughout the evening Romeo has been making pretty free with the chianti and after he leaves the party he goes round to the back of the house and with some considerable difficulty gets over the garden wall, having some vague idea of carrying on his conversation with Juliet. To his surprise and delight she presently comes out onto her bedroom balcony in her nightgown.

Well, you can guess what happens. The long and the short of it is that by the time he takes his leave, the milk is on

O Romeo, Romeo, wherefore art thou, Romeo?

the doorstep and Juliet has consented to become Mrs Montague, in spite of the fact that she now knows that Romeo belongs to that detested clan. She promises to send him a message later in the day to let him know what time she will be ready for the wedding, the two of them having agreed that there is no point in hanging about and that they might as well get married right away.

Romeo manages to get back over the wall, and then makes his way to the cell of a friendly friar called Laurence, and arranges with him for the wedding to take place that afternoon by special licence. Later in the day Juliet turns up and they are joined in wedlock by the friar, who promises to say not a word to anyone about the ceremony. It is his secret hope, poor old thing, that by uniting Capulet and Montague he may take the heat out of their quarrel. But Fate has other plans.

A little later on, a posse of Capulets walking through the Piazza dei Signori comes upon a posse of Montagues, including Romeo, footing it in the opposite direction. Snide remarks are uttered by both parties and eventually one of the Capulets called Tybalt, who is Lady Capulet's nephew and a most objectionable young man, runs his rapier through a friend of Romeo's, Mercutio, who thereupon becomes dead. Romeo himself, who up to now has taken no part in the exchange of insults, is furious at this and in return runs Tybalt through.

Now, for a Montague to kill anyone of the name of Capulet is reprehensible enough, but to kill Lady Capulet's nephew is indeed a grave matter. News of the fracas has been reported to the district Prince, who now appears and reads the riot act to both sides and ends up banishing Romeo, who by this time has made a quick flit to the cell of Friar Laurence. This, of course, puts an end to Romeo's marriage and when he hears the news he gets into a frightful state, tearing his hair, rolling about on the floor, and chewing the rush matting.

Friar Laurence is not impressed. He tells him to get up and stop being so soft. Things, he says, may not be as black as they seem, a typical piece of unctuous clerical optimism for which there is not the slightest foundation. From Romeo's point of view it seems that he might as well be dead. However, he cheers up after a while, encouraged by the suggestion (from a friar, of all people!) that before he leaves Verona for good he should secretly spend one more night of love with Juliet.

So he hangs about in the cell till it gets dark, then he creeps out to the Casa Capulet, climbs over the garden wall again (still a bit of a struggle) and up the ivy into Juliet's bedroom.

They stay together until jocund day stands tiptoe on the misty mountain top, then he climbs down again, tiptoes through the tulips, scrabbles his way over the wall and beats it across the border to Mantua.

No sooner has he gone than Lord Capulet announces his intention to find a husband for Juliet and picks one Paris as the lucky lad. Of course, Juliet dare not divulge that she is already espoused, though she does protest pretty strongly, but all to no purpose. Old Capulet is a domineering type and having made up his mind that she is going to marry Paris, he is damn well going to see that she does so. Great preparations are put in hand forthwith and Paris goes about beaming like a lighthouse.

Juliet, poor girl, is absolutely desperate. She simply does not know what to do, so she goes round to see Friar Laurence and asks his advice. Now, as well as being a friar, Laurence goes in for dispensing herbal remedies on the side and he comes up with a suggestion that Juliet should try one of his concoctions, which will lay her out for forty-eight hours with every appearance of her having passed away, after which she will be as right as rain, no unpleasant after-effects, no hangover. The Friar is taking a chance on catalepsy being mistaken by Juliet's parents for the real thing, and that seeing her to all intents and purposes devoid of any vital spark, they will have her entombed in the family vault. Meanwhile, Friar Laurence himself will send word to Romeo in Mantua about the plot and Romeo will then

Take thou this vial . . .
And this distilling liquor drink thou off

return in secret to Verona, bust open the vault during the night, by which time Juliet will have recovered her senses, and then the two of them will make tracks for Mantua together.

It is pretty clear that her senses have deserted her already or she would not for one moment entertain such a grotesque proposition when she might just as well stay hidden in Laurence's cell until Romeo is able to come and pick her up. But Laurence, who has this love of dramatizing everything, talks Juliet into going through with his rather distasteful scheme and eventually she goes home with a phial of the Friar's balsam concealed about her person.

That night she quaffs the lot and it lays her out cold. So cold that, as the Friar has predicted, it is instantly assumed that she is no more, and with almost indecent haste she is carted off to the family vault.

In the meantime Friar Laurence has sent a messenger posting off to Mantua, but before the messenger gets there, news of Juliet's engagement to Paris and then of her so-called decease has reached the ears of Romeo. He is already in a pretty bad way, the full implications of his banishment having sunk in by this time, and this is the last straw. Suicide seems the only way out. So he goes to the chemist and gets some poison and then sets off for Verona, hoping to steal a last look at Juliet before going to meet his maker. Consequently the Friar's messenger misses him.

In the middle of the night Romeo, armed with a crowbar and a lantern, arrives at the cemetery. He is just getting to work on the vault, when who should appear on the scene but Paris, carrying a bunch of flowers. It seems an odd time to choose for putting them on Juliet's tomb, but that's his affair. Seeing what Romeo is up to, he says to him, 'Stop thy unhallowed toil, vile Montague', intending to take him up and hand him over to the authorities for them to deal with him.

Romeo, knowing it means the chop for him if he is caught in Verona, and preferring his own arrangement to a state execution, defends himself against Paris, who, in a short, sharp snicker-snee, walks into the business end of Romeo's rapier and falls to the ground a dead man.

Paris has brought with him a page, who, seeing his master thus despatched, says, 'Oh Lord!' and rushes off to get assistance.

Romeo, not knowing quite what to do with Paris's corpse, thinks to himself, oh well, I suppose in the eyes of the world they were engaged, and having a proper sense of the proprieties, he lugs the corpse into the vault alongside what he takes to be Juliet's lifeless form (Tybalt, by the way, is there as well, lying on a slab of his own), and having taken leave of his loved one, Romeo downs his poison like a man.

Almost as soon as he has left the departure platform, never to return, Juliet begins to come to. Naturally, she is extremely surprised and not a little upset to see not only Romeo dead, but also Paris and Tybalt, and stabs herself with her penknife.

By this time, Paris's page having raised the alarm, a whole lot of people are rushing about the cemetery, including Lord and Lady Capulet, Lord Montague, the Prince, at least three watchmen who have suddenly appeared on the scene, Friar Laurence, and a gentleman by the name of Balthasar, who all pour into the tomb as though it were the rush hour.

Very wisely, the Prince takes the occasion to point out how ridiculous it is for the two families to go on squabbling, and, indicating the assembled corpses, the sort of thing it leads to. He urges them to pack it in and the play ends on a hopeful note of reconciliation between Capulet and Montague.

The Taming of the Shrew

In *The Taming of the Shrew* Shakespeare's understanding of human behaviour seems to have taken a walk. The idea that you can bring a hysterical bitch to heel by treating her rough is not one with which most psychiatrists would agree. The shrew in question is Katherine Minola, the elder daughter of a gentleman of private means, who lives in Padua.

His younger daughter, Bianca, is a vacuous virgin with not much to say for herself, but Katherine more than makes up for this by keeping up a stream of four-letter words ('Fool', her father, 'Jade', Bianca, 'Crab', her suitor, 'Boot', putting it in, etc.).

For some unaccountable reason, Signor Minola, who is a bit of an ass anyway, refuses to let Bianca get married until a husband has been found for Katherine. This decision looks like keeping them both on the shelf, since only someone who is not in his right mind would seem likely to marry Kate.

By great good luck, a gentleman who apparently answers to this description turns up and says he is willing to take Katherine on. The name of this dauntless character is Petruchio and he comes from Verona. Anyone else would have been glad to get back there as fast as possible after five minutes of Kate's conversation, but not Petruchio.

However, he is not quite such an idiot as this might seem to imply, having been careful to find out first of all how much Baptista Minola is willing to fork out in order to get Katherine off his hands. Needless to say, the old boy is prepared to put down a pretty large sum and on his death to make over half his lands to her husband. Thus encouraged, Petruchio sets out to woo the shrew.

As soon as she appears, he starts paying her the most idiotic compliments, which of course infuriate her and at one point she actually lashes out at him. However, Petruchio takes it all in good part, which only makes her more furious.

Presently Minola looks in, expecting to see Petruchio with a black eye, if not something worse, and is amazed to find him very perky, delighted, so he says, at the way Katherine has received him. (He breathes not a word of her having clipped him round the ear or of the frightful names she has been calling him.) He says blandly that they are to be married the following Sunday and that he will provide Kate with some sumptuous wedding gear. Kate, on the other hand, screeches that she'll see him hanged first.

Nevertheless, come Sunday a whole lot of guests turn up dressed in their uncomfortable best and wreathed in artificial grins suitable to the occasion. The parson and the cake both stand ready and Katherine is pacing ferociously about. But there is no sign of Petruchio.

Then, about half an hour later, he comes trotting in—not a word of apology—dressed in filthy old clothes and looking like nothing on earth, 'an eyesore to our solemn festival', as his future father-in-law puts it. But as Petruchio points out, Kate is marrying him, not his clothes. And by the same token he has brought her none of the finery he promised to give her, so there she is, dressed in just an ordinary old skirt and jerkin.

The ceremony gets under way and when it comes to the responses Petruchio shouts them out so loud that the parson almost jumps out of his surplice. At one point the poor old thing drops his prayer book and when he stoops down to pick it up Petruchio fetches him a tremendous clout. Then when the actual splicing is over, Petruchio having called for some wine, spews it all over the verger, whose whiskers, he says, look as though they need encouragement.

Then, with the guests all standing there, waiting with ill-concealed impatience for the sound of popping corks, Petruchio announces that they can't stop, he and Katherine must be off. So away they go, mounted on a pair of beasts that he has brought with him and which look as though he has rescued them from the glue factory.

Unfortunately, the weather has been absolutely filthy and Kate's poor old nag can hardly drag its split hooves out of the muck and mire. But Petruchio storms and yells at it all the way until eventually they arrive at his place.

Katherine

To Kate's immense relief—she is ravenous by this time and utterly weary—there is a nice little supper waiting for them. But before she can get her fork to the *antipasti* Petruchio starts flinging the food about, complaining that it isn't fit for a pig to eat, that is is an insult to offer such filthy tack to his little bride, and so on. Consequently she doesn't even get a bite and so goes supperless to bed.

In the bridal chamber Petruchio takes one look at the bed and you might think there were bugs in it from the way he carries on, tossing the bedclothes all over the room and cursing the maids for having made up the bed so badly. So in the end Kate spends her wedding night sitting up in an armchair.

And so it goes on. Petruchio finds fault with everything on the ground that nothing is good enough for her. He gets in an extremely expensive dressmaker to show her some clothes and she is thrilled with one of the dresses, but no, Petruchio says the dressmaker is a 'nit' and the dress looks like 'an apple tart'. So in the end Kate gets no clothes, as well as having had no food or sleep. By this time the poor girl is more or less a wreck, but Petruchio takes not a blind bit of notice and carries on as before.

A few days later he decides that they shall ride over to Minola's villa for dinner. And just to see whether Kate has learnt her lesson, he tries to make out that the sun overhead is the moon, to which she dutifully agrees, being absolutely fed up by this time. But she can't win. 'You lie,' he says, 'it is the blessed sun!' So she says all right, then, it's the sun.

The next thing is that they meet an old-age pensioner tottering along the road and Petruchio addresses him as though he were a girl. So Kate does the same, calling him a 'young budding virgin'. The pensioner, of course, thinks they are both sozzled, but they have a bit of a talk and presently it turns out that the old fellow is the father of a youth called Lucentio, who is about to marry Bianca. So all three of them go along to Minola's together, and arrive very conveniently just in time for the wedding.

Staying in the house for the weekend is another married

Away thou rag, thou quantity, thou remnant

couple, a chap called Hortensio and his wife, who is mentioned merely (and it would seem rather prematurely) as being a widow.

After dinner, when the ladies have gone upstairs, leaving the men to their *strega*, the others twit Petruchio with having married a shrew, but Petruchio denies this and offers to lay a bet that of the three brides, Kate is the most obedient. So Lucentio sends one of the men servants to tell Bianca to come down. The man returns to say that if Lucentio wants to see her, he can jolly well go up to the drawing room.

So then Hortensio sends the man up to bring down his wife, the so-called widow. But the result is the same. Of course, Petruchio is looking pretty smug by this time, though both the others naturally think he hasn't got a chance. Conceive of their amazement, therefore, when in answer to a message that Petruchio has sent upstairs, Katherine meekly appears and says that the other two girls are sitting having a heart-to-heart on the drawing-room fender.

Petruchio orders her to go up and fetch them down and when in their own good time they consent to appear, he tells her to explain to them where the path of duty lies, *ie*, in obedience to their husbands. And just to prove Kate's acquiescence in this policy, he says he doesn't like her hat, it looks perfectly awful, and he tells her to take it off and jump on it. And so humble has the poor idiotic girl become that she obeys him. So much for Women's Lib.

The Merry Wives of Windsor

This play provides a warning to a not uncommon type of man, the middle-aged gent who sees himself, as the years advance, still acting the role of the gay flaneur that he has played for so long in his imagination.

Such a man is Sir John Falstaff, who leads a shabby-genteel life, doing nothing in particular but boasting, and boozing. He also does a bit of poaching on the side, aided and abetted by three perfectly frightful ex-army friends, Bardolph, Nym and Pistol.

Falstaff, always on the make, and with an infinite capacity for self-delusion, thinks he sees a way to pick up some easy money by seducing a woman called Mrs Ford. She is a pleasant, suburban lady, quite well-off and married to a rather dull man called Frank Ford. She can hardly be described as glamorous and is certainly not in her first youth, yet merely on the strength of her having been agreeable to him in casual conversation, Falstaff has let his imagination run riot. He announces to his three grotty friends that Mrs Ford is wildly attracted to him, that he has only to lift his little finger and she will leap into bed with him, and then, as she controls the purse-strings of the Ford household, he need never want for money.

The improbability of this fantasy is enhanced when he tells an exactly similar story about a friend of Mrs Ford's, Meg Page. A dawning suspicion on the part of Nym and Pistol that Falstaff may be out of his mind is confirmed when he says he has written to both ladies, suggesting an affair with each of them and orders Nym and Pistol to deliver the letters. He usually treats them either like servants or as imbeciles and they have put up with it so far because of what they have been able to get out of him. But they both draw the line at acting as Falstaff's pimps. Absolutely furious at their refusal, he gets his page Robin to deliver the letters instead, and then he stumps off. Nym is fed up to the teeth with Falstaff by this time, and he decides to go and tell Mr Page what the old goat is up to.

Mrs Ford is reading the letter delivered by Robin when quite unexpectedly Mrs Page calls. They are both pretty annoyed, but can see that the situation has its funny side, so instead of making heavy weather of it, they decide to say nothing to their husbands, but to take it out of Falstaff in their own way.

They get hold of a local busybody, Mrs Nell Quickly, and having promised to make it worth her while, they send her round to Falstaff with a message. She tells him that although Mrs Ford has refused numerous offers of seduction from various members of the Establishment, including one or two peers, and she has always remained faithful to her husband, she finds Falstaff irresistible. If he likes to take advantage of the fact, she will be alone that night between ten and eleven.

There is also a message in similar terms from Mrs Page, faithful ere now to her husband, a respectable nonentity called George Page. She, too, hopes to find some way of arranging an assignation, if Falstaff will allow young Robin to act as their go-between.

While all this is going on, Nym and Pistol go round to Frank Page's house, where George and Frank are together, and reveal Falstaff's plan. In the light of personal experience and the ages of their wives, both husbands are sceptical about Nym's story, but just in case, George decides to test the strength of it.

Disguised as someone called Brook—why disguised, God knows, as neither of them know each other—George goes to see Falstaff, who seems not in the least surprised that a complete stranger should tell him he is passionately in love with Mrs Ford, but hasn't the nerve to do anything about it. The stranger proposes that Falstaff should first broach the keg, *ie*, Mrs Ford, thus laying her open to blackmail, and that he himself should then step in and gain his ends by threatening to expose her. On the promise of being well rewarded, Falstaff agrees.

Again, the two ladies get together. Mrs Ford tells the servants they are to stand by to take the laundry and chuck it in a ditch at Datchet. She gives no explanation of this order and the servants retire, completely mystified.

Mistress Ford, by my troth you are very well met

Next, little Robin arrives and soon it becomes evident that by the promise of some new gear he has been suborned by the two ladies into betraying his master, whose arrival he has come to announce. When the old buck shows up, Mrs Page makes herself scarce.

The fat knight loses no time in getting down to his agreeable task and is already tampering with Mrs Ford's stays when Robin rushes in to say Mrs Page is on her way up. So Falstaff nips behind the arras, where of course he can hear everything that is said.

Mrs Page, putting up a tremendous act of alarm and despondency, begs Mrs Ford, in case she should be hiding a lover, to get rid of him *subito*, because George Ford is on his way home with a search party, having heard that a man is concealed in the house.

Falstaff jumps out when he hears this, and Mrs Page lets off a well-rehearsed scream. There is no time for explanations. Falstaff is shoved into the laundry basket and the servants are instructed to do as they have been told.

Eventually, George marches in and while he and his pals search the house, the two ladies, secretly convulsed, decide to take another crack at Falstaff. So Mrs Page calls to see him and says that if he will present himself at Mrs Ford's between eight and nine, George will be out again.

'I will visit her . . . and bid her think what a man is,' says Falstaff.

Later on, Ford, again disguised as Brook, calls on him to find out how he is doing. Falstaff, after telling him what happened and how it ended with his being dumped in a stinking ditch, swears he is ready to have another go and in fact has arranged a new assignation, ''twixt eight and nine'.

At the appointed hour he is starting his preliminary fondling of Mrs Ford when again the alarm is raised. This time Falstaff's only way of escape is in disguise, as 'the fat woman of Brainford', Mrs Ford's maid's aunt, whom Ford detests, and when the knight appears in this disguise, Ford gives him a tremendous whacking.

After this, both wives tell their husbands the whole

*I am here a **Windsor** stag, and the fattest, **I** think, i' the forest*

story and it is decided that Falstaff shall be given the *coup de grâce* that night in Windsor Forest. He is persuaded by a further message to turn up there at midnight, arrayed like Herne the Hunter, looking a complete idiot with antlers on his head. But instead of the alfresco seduction scene he has anticipated, he is tormented by a gang of 'fairies' (in reality, juvenile relations of the Fords and the Pages) and his fingers are toasted with candles. The two husbands, relieved to find themselves not the cuckolds they had suspected, forgive the old man and in the end cart him off to bury his sorrows and his nose in a warm posset.

The Merchant of Venice

It is difficult to tell the story of *The Merchant of Venice* without incurring some suspicion of being antisemitic. But the fault is Shakespeare's. In Shylock he created such a frightful stinker that no one could possibly find him anything but repulsive, mean and greedy.

This human slug—he is a well-to-do money-lender—lives in Venice. Now, among the gilded youths who hang about in Harry's Bar or sit sipping their *espressi* in the Piazza, are Antonio and Bassanio. At quite an early age, Antonio, who is decidedly the smarter of the two, has made a packet out of shipping. But Bassanio, an attractive layabout, far from making a packet, has caught one, having chucked away a fortune simply through living it up, and when the play opens he is standing delicately poised on his beam-ends. He is in a desperate state—so desperate, in fact, that he has decided there is nothing for it but to marry a rich girl. Some might think worse could befall, but Bassanio has much enjoyed the fruits of being a bachelor, though these have now become a bit sour.

His roving eye has alighted on a very nice girl called Portia, whose immensely wealthy Papa has conveniently passed away only a little while earlier, leaving her disgustingly rich.

From his own fortune Bassanio has nothing left, not even credit, and as he now looks pathetically down-at-heel, he asks Antonio to lend him three thousand ducats so that he can kit himself out to make the right impression on Portia. Somewhat surprisingly, Antonio himself is in rather a tight corner at this particular moment; a temporary embarrassment till his ship—or rather, ships—come home. So he says, 'Let's go round to the old Jew and I'll see if I can raise the wind.'

Unfortunately, Shylock absolutely detests Antonio, because the lad never stops pulling his leg about the exorbitant rates of interest that he charges, so now the old vulture thinks he has spotted a way of getting his own back. He abandons his usual slimy role of being the injured party and pretends to forgive all, even to make a joke of the transaction.

The joke, a pretty fair example of Shylock's sense of humour, is that Antonio should offer a pound of his own adipose tissue as security for three thousand ducats, to be lent for three months (at some colossal percentage, of course) and that a formal bond or agreement on these terms should be drawn up and signed by both parties.

To do Bassanio justice, he doesn't trust Shylock and begs Antonio to call off the deal. But Antonio says, of course not. He says 'my ships come home a month before the day', and so he signs the bond and the Jew hands over the money, which Antonio then gives to his friend.

A little later, Bassanio, dressed to kill, goes out to Portia's place in the country and proposes to her. He is quite straightforward about the situation. He says, 'I'll tell you frankly, I haven't got a bean. All I can offer is my high birth and my noble ancestry.'

Now, if Portia has a fault it is that she is a bit of a social snob, but at the same time she finds Bassanio really very attractive, so she says okay, and she gives him an engagement ring, because of course he can't afford one for her, and he swears that he will never part with it.

At this point a messenger comes rushing on with a letter from Antonio. Bassanio reads it, then turns to Portia and says, 'Here are a few of the unpleasant'st words that ever blotted paper', which is putting it mildly, because it appears that Antonio's entire merchant fleet has been sunk (and you can bet there were some pretty long faces at Lloyd's when the news came through), but worse still, Shylock is bringing an action for the enforcement of his claim against Antonio.

Bassanio now has to explain to Portia about the bond and Antonio's reason for signing it. He has at least had the decency not to mention it to her before, but she takes it all in her stride and when Bassanio says he must go and see Antonio straight away, she agrees.

After Bassanio has left her, she thinks about the situation for a while and then she gets an idea. She hasn't much confidence in Antonio's lawyer, so she persuades the old man to

Well Shylock, shall we be beholden to you?

let her appear in court as Antonio's counsel and for her maid Nerissa to act as her clerk. However, as the success of this arrangement must depend on Antonio and Bassanio both failing to penetrate her disguise, or else the game will be given away, the chances of the trick coming off look pretty slender.

Do not, however, underestimate the author's capacity for working miracles. Portia marches into court dressed in a black gown and with an Italian barrister's toque perched on the top of her head, and this, believe it or not, is sufficient for both Antonio and Bassanio to be completely taken in, as they are by the appearance of Nerissa, tagging along behind dressed as Portia's clerk.

'Who on earth is this?' says the judge, scarcely able to believe that the cherubic individual standing before him is old enough to appear in a court of law.

'I am Doctor Balthazar,' says Portia, bold as brass. 'I appear, me lord, for the defendant.'

'Very well,' says the judge, passing his hand over his face to hide an incipient grin. 'Proceed.'

So the case begins, and soon the usual incomprehensible arguments are in full spate, with one side quoting *Medici v. Machiavelli DB XVII (1512)* and the other citing *23 Gorgonzola, c.162 (1578)*, while the judge tries to pretend he is not yawning.

Presently Portia gets up to make a statement. What she says in effect is that her client does not propose to offer a defence and she invites Shylock to sharpen his carving knife and get to work.

'But,' she says, 'I wish to point out on behalf of my client that the bond stipulates the removal of flesh only.'

At this point the judge intervenes.

'Mr Balthazar, do I take it that in these circumstances it is your intention to apply to the court for an *ex parte* injunction?'

'With respect, me lord, no. At this stage only for a writ of *certiorari.*'

'You had better make haste then, Mr Balthazar. If the

plaintiff should succeed, *habeas corpus*, if it be required, may be impossible to sustain. Proceed.'

'The bond does not say anything about blood,' says Portia, and she reminds the court that for a Jew to shed the blood of a Christian is an offence punishable by forfeiture of the assailant's lands and goods.

Shylock, in the box, is gnashing his gums at being taken for a ride by, as it seems, this young whipper-snapper of a barrister, who can only just have passed his finals. However, he says, 'Very well, I'll take the ducats instead.'

'You'll do no such thing,' says Portia, 'There's nothing in the bond about ducats, only flesh. So start carving.'

'One moment,' says the judge. 'Mr Shylock, have you any experience in vivisection?'

'None whatever, me lord.'

'I thought not.' The judge leans back with a faint smirk on his face. 'Proceed, Mr Balthazar.'

Portia sticks to her point, but Shylock still pleads to be allowed to settle for the cash and eventually Portia switches her argument.

'You knew very well, did you not, that it would be an impossibility for you to carve your pound of rump steak from my client without endangering his life?'

Shylock doesn't answer, just stands there squirming.

'I put it to you that you were, in fact, were you not, conspiring against my client's life?' Then Portia says to the judge, 'I would venture to say, me lord, that in so doing the plaintiff has been guilty *a priori* of committing a capital offence.'

'What's that? What about gorgonzola?' the judge asks, waking up with a start, 'I am not with you, Mr Balthazar.'

Portia explains the situation and eventually judgement is given for Antonio, who gets half of Shylock's money, and so, with the other half awarded in costs, the Jew is faced with the prospect of becoming a pauper.

But Antonio saves the old man's bacon (he doesn't, of course, use this un-kosher metaphor) by offering to give back the money if Shylock will consent to his daughter marrying a friend of Antonio's, which the old tight-wad has hitherto forbidden. So what can Shylock do but agree? Then the judge says that if Shylock will become a Christian, the court will remit the order for costs. Well, of course, that is rather a different kettle of fish, so Shylock says he'll go home and think about it.

The judge then asks Portia if she will come out to dinner with him (presumably he suspects she is not all she seems to be), but Portia says no, and who shall blame her?

Bassanio now approaches Portia—she, don't forget, is the girl he is engaged to—and staring her full in the face without apparently having the faintest idea who she is, he offers her, as a fee, the three thousand ducats that Antonio has lent him.

Portia at first refuses to take anything, then she says, 'Well, all right, if you insist, give me those old gloves you're wearing!' (This is all part of a trick to test him.) So Bassanio whips them off, disclosing the ring that Portia has given him.

'Oh,' she says, 'How about the ring? I rather like that.'

Bassanio says it is the one thing he can't part with because he has vowed never to give it away. Portia pretends to be rather annoyed at this. 'You're not very grateful,' she says, and she marches off with Nerissa and they both go home.

Presently Antonio and Bassanio turn up at the house in a state of tremendous jubilation. While they are all congratulating themselves, Nerissa suddenly starts a scene. (What she is doing hanging about in the *salone* instead of being upstairs turning down the beds and laying out Portia's nightgown is one of those things that is never explained.) She accuses her boy friend, Gratiano, who is only there because he happens to be an acquaintance of Antonio's, of giving away a ring which he, like Bassanio, had promised never to part with. The explanation is, of course, that he has imitated Bassanio and given the ring in court to Balthazar's 'clerk' as a *piccolo dono* (not recognizing Nerissa, needless to state).

Portia sides with Nerissa and goes for Gratiano, who in self-defence cites the parallel of Bassanio giving away *his*

Sir, I entreat you home with me to dinner

ring. This really puts the cat among the pigeons. Portia turns on Bassanio like a fire-hose, until Antonio steps in and points out that the ring was given away to save his life and that he is quite sure Bassanio wouldn't do such a thing for any other reason.

'Then you shall be his surety,' Portia says. 'Give him this ring.' And she hands over the one that Bassanio gave her in court. When he sees it his eyes bug out.

'By heaven,' he says, 'it is the same I gave the doctor.'

'It's what the doctor ordered,' says Portia, and then she explains the whole thing.

In the middle of it, while they are all rolling about with laughter, Portia slips a note to Antonio. She doesn't say where it came from (another of those things you are left to guess), but it brings the good news that through an idiotic mistake on somebody's part, the news about Antonio's shipping disaster is absolutely untrue, the whole fleet is safe and sound. So everybody is delighted. Bassanio has got his Portia, Nerissa has got her Gratiano, Antonio has got his ducats, and Shylock has got a kick up the backside.

111

A House in Stratford upon Avon, in u